W9-ASF-272

THE NEW EYES OF THE SCIENTIST

THE NEW EYES OF THE SCIENTIST

BY THOMAS H. METOS

Franklin Watts / An Impact Book
New York / London / Toronto / Sydney / 1988

ST. PHILIP'S COLLEGE LIBRARY.

THE NEW EYES OF THE SCIENTIST

BY THOMAS H. METOS

Library of Congress Cataloging-in-Publication Data
Metos, Thomas H.
The new eyes of the scientist / by Thomas H. Metos.
p.   cm. — (An Impact book)
Bibliography: p.
Includes index.
Summary: Discusses how new visual and optical technology
has helped expand the world of the scientist in giving new
tools to perform research experiments and stretch our knowledge of space.
ISBN 0-531-10609-8
1. Scientific apparatus and instruments—Juvenile literature.
2. Research—Methodology—Juvenile literature.   3. Optical
instruments—Juvenile literature. [1. Scientific apparatus and
instruments.   2. Optical instruments.]   I. Title.
Q185.3.M47   1988
502'.8—dc19   88-14263   CIP   AC

Copyright © 1988 by Thomas H. Metos
All rights reserved
Printed in the United States of America
5   4   3   2   1

Illustrations by Vantage Art

Photographs courtesy of: Oakridge National Laboratory: pp. 19 (top), 31, 34, 35, 37, 38, 48, 49; *Photomicrography Designs and Patterns*, Louis R. Wolberg, Dover Publications, Inc., New York, © 1974: p. 19 (bottom); Argonne National Laboratory: p. 46; Oak Ridge Associated Universities: p. 57; Brookhaven National Laboratory: pp. 68, 69; Photo Researchers, Inc.: pp. 74 (Will & Deni McIntyre © 1987), 75 (Hank Morgan/Science Source), 77 (Robert Goldstein), 92 (Royal Astronomical Society), 94 (Allen Madans); University of Arizona: pp. 89, 104; CARA: pp. 101, 102; NASA: pp. 113, 114.

086993

CONTENTS

Introduction
11

Chapter One
A New Pair of Glasses
15

Chapter Two
TEMs, SEMs, and Other
Electron Microscopes
27

Chapter Three
A Closer View of Our Bodies
53

CONTENTS

Chapter Four
Expanding Medical Imaging
71

Chapter Five
Eyes on Space
83

Chapter Six
Eyes in Space
107

Source Notes 135

Index 139

THE NEW EYES OF THE SCIENTIST

INTRODUCTION

During recent years, we have been able—for the first time—to see atoms, viruses, and the molecules that make up the human gene. We are now able to see human organs at work. Looking into space we are able to view the ice rings of Saturn and the pitch-black rings of Uranus. We routinely see and precisely map the land masses and oceans of the world. We can actually see from outer space the temperatures, wind flows, pollutants, health of plants, and patterns of climate and erosion. All of this is possible because of the invention and continued refinement of new scientific "eyes."

Today these new eyes—instruments like electron microscopes, space probes, super-telescopes, and medical imaging machines—are changing our knowledge of the world and the universe. And they are changing our lives.

ST. PHILIP'S COLLEGE LIBRARY.

In laboratories and hospitals, technicians and doctors use this new equipment to discover, treat, and often cure human diseases that previously were either untreatable or not detected until it was too late to save the patient. For example, until the early 1970s, the only way that doctors could normally examine a patient's brain was through the use of three techniques. Two of these combined the use of conventional X rays with either the injecting of a dye in the bloodstream or the pumping of air into a patient's spinal cord to displace brain fluid. These two techniques were not always successful in giving the physician a definitive view of the brain. The third option was to actually cut open the patient's skull and expose the brain for examination. Today, the interior of the human body can be viewed by physicians through the use of a variety of machines and techniques, with much less discomfort and danger to the patient while giving the physician an image of the body never before possible.

Some inventions and refinements are dependent upon the application of other instruments, especially computers. Often, the giant leaps in the capabilities of scientific instruments are a result of powerful, intelligent computers that direct, monitor, and manipulate the data of the instrument being used. Without the computer, many of the new medical imaging machines would not have been possible.

On an increasingly frequent basis other powerful new tools are being adapted to scientific, medical, and defense purposes. The laser, coupled with fluorescent imaging, is now being used to study biological specimens. Sensors that measure surface reactions on a microsecond time scale are being used to analyze, at very high resolutions, objects subject to radiation. Some of the new telescopes use sensors to manipulate several mirrors in concert to control the amount and kind of light being gathered.

During the next twenty years, medical scientists may be able, through the use of their new machines, or eyes, to discover ways of lengthening our lives and curing diseases that have plagued humankind. Other scientists may be able to prove whether there is a planet in our solar system beyond Pluto and even discover how the universe was formed. Others may be able to accurately forecast weather and changes in climate and find new sources of minerals on Earth.

In the following pages, we will look at some of these new machines that enable us to see things we never could before. The technology is complex and often difficult for the layperson to grasp, but the contribution these machines are making to our storehouse of knowledge is enormous—and well worth examination.

ONE

A NEW PAIR OF GLASSES

Magnifying lenses of some type or another may have been used by humans for thousands of years, but it was not until the early 1600s that modern-day microscopy had its beginnings. The work of such pioneers as Johannes Kepler (1571–1630), René Descartes (1596–1650), and especially the Englishman Robert Hooke (1635–1703) laid the groundwork for the optical microscope. Descartes, in his famous book *Dioptrique* published in 1607, shows two simple types of microscopes he designed. Hooke was the first to study shaved sections of objects, using several different techniques to illuminate the object to be viewed.

Marcello Malpighi (1628–1694), Christopher Wren (1632–1723), and Jan Swammerdam (1637–1680) further refined the techniques of microscopy through the use of mounting and specimen plates and the staining techniques of dissection. It was Antoni van Leeuwenhoek (1632–1723), a Dutch cloth merchant, who was the first person to mass-produce microscopes. Van Leeuwenhoek's instruments were crude affairs, but his lenses were precision-made. Other builders of microscopes followed, making it possible for almost anyone interested in using a microscope to buy one and study specimens.

Although van Leeuwenhoek is responsible for the mass production of microscopes, his greatest contribution was his study of microorganisms, for which he is credited as being the founder of microbiology. His observations and drawings of bacteria and other microorganisms set the stage for the study of microbes and their relationship to disease.

As the interest in microscopy grew, innovations and refinements soon followed—compound lenses, better focusing devices, and achromatic lenses (lenses in which different glasses are combined in such a way as to render the lenses virtually free from unwanted colors), for example. It seemed that there would be no end to improvement of the optical microscope and its ability to see smaller and smaller details. However, in the 1870s, Ernst Abbe (1852–1911), a German physicist who was a partner in the famous optical works of Carl Zeiss, predicted that the optical microscope would never be able to show details smaller than half the wavelength of light, or about 250 nanometers (abbreviated as nm). In essence, this limits the magnification of the optical microscope to no more than 2,000 times, or $1/125,000$ of an inch. Because of this limitation, scientists turned their attention to other possible ways of magnifying details of objects.

DEVELOPMENT OF THE ELECTRON MICROSCOPE

About the same time that Abbe was cautioning that the optical microscope did indeed have its limits, research was being carried out in Germany on cathode-ray tubes, which would later be the basis for the electron microscope.[1]

Since the mid-1850s, electrical engineers had experimented with cathode-ray tubes. These tubes consisted of electrodes sealed in a glass tube after the air had been evacuated. The engineers who experimented with these tubes knew that the tubes emitted rays in a linear fashion and that these rays could be concentrated by electrical fields. Although the "cathode rays," as they were known at that time, were invisible, they became visible upon striking a fluorescent screen. In 1897, the English physicist Joseph J. Thomson (1856–1940) was able to demonstrate that these cathode rays were streams of negatively charged ions that he called "electrons."

Thomson's work caused a great deal of interest among scientists. Other researchers soon found that the electron beam could be concentrated through the use of an electromagnet or electrostatic field. In 1924, a French physicist, Louis de Broglie (1892–1987), proposed that an electron was not only a negatively charged particle but was also a form of wave motion. This important concept led to the finding that a suitably shaped magnetic field could be used as a lens in an electron microscope. During the next seven years, several other researchers experimented with cathode-ray tubes, and in 1931 the German scientists Max Knoll and Ernst Ruska developed the first electron microscope. This machine's image could only be magnified seventeen times and could only produce the image of the cathode of the tube.

In 1933, Ruska built a second microscope which is the antecedent of modern-day electron microscopes. In Ruska's microscope the electrons were accelerated by 75,000 volts of electricity applied to the anode. Three lenses— one acting as a condenser lens and two magnifying, or imaging, lenses—were shrouded in iron and water-cooled. Specimens were mounted horizontally in a column, which could be rotated from outside the vacuum. The first pictures of magnified specimens were taken from outside the fluorescent screen; later an internal camera was housed in the microscope.

The first specimens Ruska examined were of aluminum foil and cotton fibers. These specimens were burned up by the intensity of the beams, but not before pictures were taken with a resolution of around 500 angstroms. (An angstrom is a unit of wavelength of light equal to one ten-billionth of a meter, and is abbreviated as Å.) A year later, two other German scientists successfully produced pictures of parts of a housefly with a resolution of about 400 Å, a resolution about five times better than available with an optical microscope.

During the next several years, improved electron microscopes were developed by scientists around the world. In 1936, the first commercial electron microscope was built in England, and shortly after, commercial electron microscopes were built in Germany and the United States. World War II slowed development work on electron microscopes, but a major breakthrough came in 1946 with the introduction of the stigmator lens, which compensated for the microscope's astigmatism, or the inability of the objective lens to converge electron beams equally. More and more powerful machines became available until, today, we have electron microscopes capable of magnifying an incredible 20 million times.[2]

Top: *a transmission electron microscope assures productions of highest resolution images.*Bottom: *A photomicrograph of the leg of a housefly.*

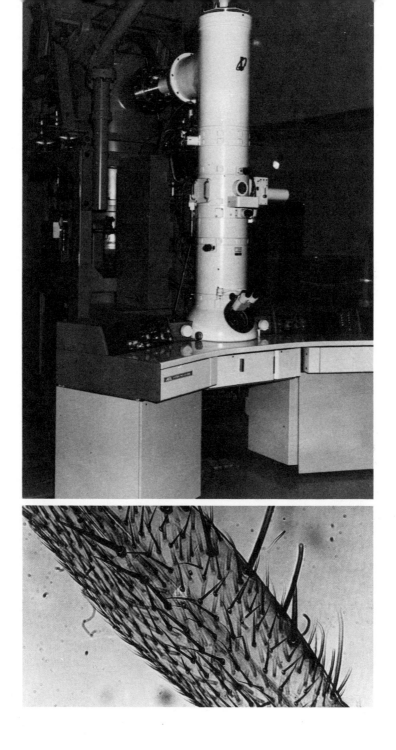

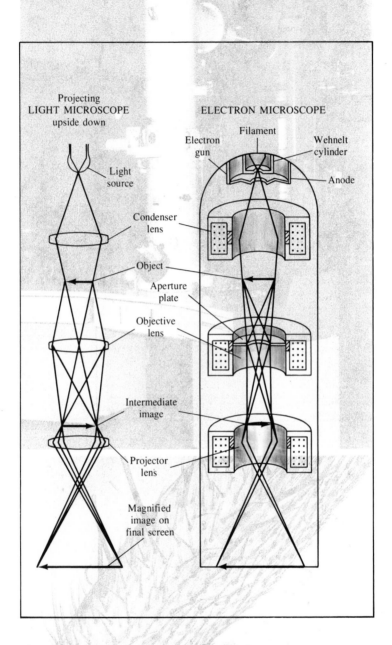

Figure 1. The optical microscope, left, is reversed to show its similarity to the transmission electron microscope, right.

HOW ELECTRON MICROSCOPES WORK

Today's transmission electron microscope consists of essentially the same components as Ruska's seminal machine. They are: (1) the electron gun, (2) the image-producing system, and (3) the image-recording system.

The electron gun, the source of the electrons, is a heated, V-shaped pointed filament of tungsten surrounded by a shield or open cylinder called the Wehnelt cylinder (see fig. 2). The tip of the filament is either at or just

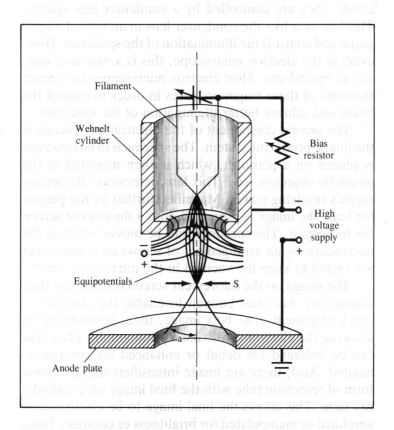

Filament

Wehnelt cylinder

Bias resistor

High voltage supply

Equipotentials

S

a

Anode plate

Figure 2. Self-biased electron gun, showing lens-type constriction of the beam to a focal spot S.

above the opening of the cylinder. To allow for fine adjustment and focusing of the beam emitted by the electron gun, the cathode (−) often has a bias-resistor, or, because of the negative potential between the shield and the filament, it may be self-biasing. The other part of the gun is an anode (+), which is a positively charged disk with a hole in the center on the axis of the microscope's column. The electrons, then, leave the cathode and are accelerated toward the anode, where they pass through the hole and on along the tube, like water from a hose.

As the electrons are narrowed into a beam by the anode, they are controlled by a condenser lens system. This lens acts like the condenser lens in an optical microscope and controls the illumination of the specimen. However, in the electron microscope, this is a magnetic lens, not an optical one. Most electron microscopes have more than one of these magnetic lenses in order to control the beam and achieve better illumination of the specimen.

The second component of the electron microscope is the image-producing system. The specimen to be observed is placed on a platform, which is then mounted in the magnetic objective lens. This lens determines the microscope's resolving power. Magnified further by the projector lens, the image is projected onto a fluorescent screen for inspection. The specimen can be moved while in the microscope by an arrangement of screws and cranks that are sealed to keep the vacuum in the microscope intact.

The image on the fluorescent screen is often less than satisfactory, but clear enough to enable the observer to check alignment. The best image, then, is produced by allowing the electrons to strike a photographic plate that can be enlarged for detail or enhanced for contrast as needed. Also, there are image intensifiers that use some form of television tube with the final image on a cathode-ray tube. This allows the final image to be electronically amplified or manipulated for brightness or contrast. Thus, the full magnitude of electron microscopes can be utilized in examining specimens.

The transmission electron microscope does have several limitations. One, as previously discussed, is in getting clear and precise resolution. Another is that because of the absence of air in the column of the microscope, specimens containing volatile substances are dessicated or destroyed. The problem of dealing with the vacuum was solved by using an air lock for the platform of the microscope. This allows for specimens to be placed in and removed from the column without disturbing the vacuum in the rest of the column. A third problem is that the electrons themselves, as they penetrate the specimen, may also destroy the specimen because of the heat generated by their passage. For example, if a specimen contained water, the combination of the vacuum and the heat of the electrons would cause the specimen to explode or burn and be rendered unusable, as happened in the early experiments of Ruska.[3]

The actual preparation of the specimen to be viewed under the electron microscope turned out to be a vitally important step, and one that presented a number of problems, too. Improperly prepared, the specimen might be burned or destroyed, or impurities might be introduced into the microscope column. But the most immediate problem was that of cutting a slice of the specimen for viewing. Early specimen preparations were done using the basic technique that had been developed for optical microscopes, using a steel microtome knife. This method proved most unsatisfactory because the thin and fragile sections were cut dry and proved almost impossible to remove from the knife. The use of water to float the sections off the steel knife, however, soon caused the knife edge to rust and become blunted.

A fortunate accident in a laboratory solved the problem. When a sheet of plate glass was dropped, a laboratory worker immediately thought to experiment with the fragments of the glass to see if they would serve as suitable knives. They did. When water was used to float a specimen off the edge of the glass, the glass edge did not corrode and become blunted. (In 1956, a Venezuelan millionaire, Humberto Fernandez-Moran, sponsored the development of the diamond knife. He traveled around the world giving away diamond knives to electron-microscope laboratories. Unfortunately, a revolution in Venezuela caused him to go into exile and brought a stop to the free knives. A few years later, his associates were able to start production again—for a price, however.)[4]

WHAT CAN BE SEEN

The process of preparing the specimens depends upon the type of specimen to be examined and the type of examination desired. Biological specimens are prepared much like those for observation in an optical microscope. The specimen is fixed and dried and embedded in resin. It is then placed in a mount, and the knife, glass or diamond, cuts a very thin slice of the specimen, which is floated onto a surface of distilled water. The slice is then picked up from the surface on a copper grid, dried, and placed directly into the electron microscope for examination.

Many kinds of materials may be examined with an electron microscope, and many are prepared differently from the procedure used for biological specimens. In some cases, the specimen is replicated or duplicated, usually on a thin coating of carbon, because carbon is heat and electrostatically conducting and the specimen is not. Usually the specimen is coated first with a solution of amyl acetate to clean the surface. Then the surface is coated with several layers of amyl acetate to build up the base of the specimen. The negative replica is then stripped from the specimen, and a layer of evaporated carbon is applied to the replica by the use of a carbon arc to make it an exact replica of the specimen. If greater contrast is needed, a thin layer of evaporated metal may be applied to the replica to cause the irregularities to be highlighted.

Another way of examining surfaces is to use a "negative staining" technique. In examining viruses, for example, the specimen is surrounded by salts of a metal that are opaque to the electron beam. When the specimen is examined in the microscope, a negative image results with the shape of the specimen outlined in very sharp relief. Powders of some substances, such as dry yeast, need not be treated in this manner. They are placed on polystyrene disks, as are other specimens that are sensitive to solvent, covered with a weighted glass, and heated for five minutes at 329° F (165° C). The specimen, after cooling, is subjected to a carbon arc in a vacuum to coat the surface to produce a replica.

Biological specimens might also be stained in situations where contrast is needed. The specimen will be sliced, and at the fixation stage, osmium tetroxide is added to provide the appropriate electron density. Another method of staining is to float the specimen, when it is on the grid, in a solution of lead or uranyl salts. After washing and drying the specimen, it is ready for examination.

Metal specimens may be examined by using an extremely thin foil of the metal so that the electrons will penetrate the metal. To examine plastic, rubber, and some biological specimens under the microscope, samples may be frozen and then sliced in order to get a thin enough specimen for replication.[5]

TWO

TEMS, SEMS, AND OTHER ELECTRON MICROSCOPES

The first electron microscopes were called transmission electron microscopes (TEMs). As we have seen, they worked much like an optical, or light, microscope, except that electrons were the source of illumination and passed through the specimen to produce an image. Soon it became apparent that as marvelous as the TEM was in producing images far beyond the limits of the optical microscope, it had severe limitations.

First was the problem of using specimens that were volatile in nature. The heat of the electron beams would either decompose or burn up the delicate microscope specimen. This is turn would contaminate the interior of the microscope, and in an electron microscope cleanliness is a must. Second, the necessity of having the interior column of the microscope under vacuum and the placing of the specimen in this vacuum generally prohibits the use of live specimens. Third, the process of preparing the specimen, the thinness needed, the drying of it, and placing it in a vacuum could alter the character of the specimen. Fourth, the final image of the TEM is only two-dimensional. Although the specimen may be tilted to produce stereoscopic images, the application of this technique is limited. Fifth, often in imaging biological specimens, the chemicals used in the preparation of the specimen alter its atomic makeup.[6]

Because of these limitations, scientists began to look for alternatives to the TEM. In 1937, development began on the scanning electron microscope (SEM). As opposed to the TEM, the SEM was designed to study the surface of a specimen directly. The SEM uses a focused beam of electrons as an electron probe that scans over the specimen in a regular manner (fig. 3). The action of the beam striking the specimen causes emissions of secondary electrons, backscattered electrons, X rays, and photons. These emissions are then fed to a scintillator crystal that produces tiny flashes of light, which in turn activate a photomultiplier tube that amplifies the tiny flashes of light.

The signals are then displayed on a cathode-ray tube. Each point of brightness on the cathode-ray tube reflects a point-by-point correlation with the secondary electrons emitted from the specimen. The picture on the tube, like a television tube, is made up of scanner, or raster, lines. These lines limit the degree of magnification available. However, because the image is produced outside the vacuum of the microscope, photomicrography with quick developing (Polaroid) film is easily accomplished.

One of the greatest advantages of the SEM over the TEM is in the area of specimen preparation. In many cases, there is no need for special preparation, and large specimens can be accommodated. If the surface of the

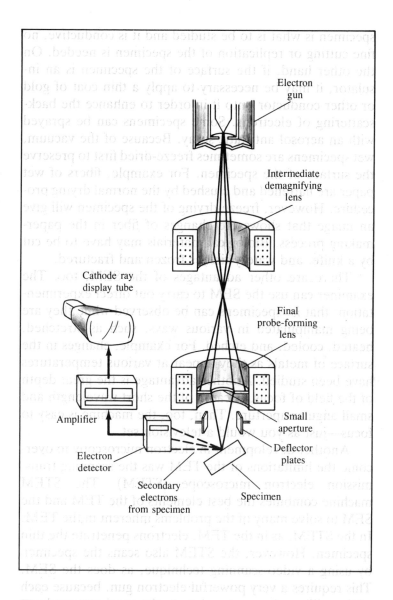

Figure 3. The scanning electron microscope uses a focused beam of electrons as an electron probe that scans over the specimen in a regular manner.

specimen is what is to be studied and it is conductive, no fine cutting or replication of the specimen is needed. On the other hand, if the surface of the specimen is an insulator, it may be necessary to apply a thin coat of gold or other conductor onto it in order to enhance the backscattering of electrons. Some specimens can be sprayed with an aerosol antistatic spray. Because of the vacuum, wet specimens are sometimes freeze-dried first to preserve the surface of the specimen. For example, fibers of wet paper are flattened and crushed by the normal drying procedure. However, freeze-drying of the specimen will give an image that shows the changes of fiber in the papermaking process. Biological materials may have to be cut by a knife, and watery tissues frozen and fractured.

There are other advantages of the SEM, too. The examiner can use the SEM to carry out direct experimentation; that is, specimens can be observed while they are being manipulated in various ways, such as stretched, heated, cooled, and etched. For example, changes in the surface of metals as they appear at various temperatures have been studied. Another advantage is the great depth of the field of focus, because of the short wavelength and small angular aperture. Then, too, the machine is easy to focus—just as you would a television set.

Another development in electron microscopy to overcome the limitations of the TEM was the scanning transmission electron microscope (STEM). The STEM machine combines the best elements of the TEM and the SEM to solve many of the problems inherent in the TEM. In the STEM, as in the TEM, electrons penetrate the thin specimen. However, the STEM also scans the specimen by using a video-scanning technique, as does the SEM. This requires a very powerful electron gun, because each of the million or so scan points on the specimen produces a weak backscatter signal.

The power of the STEM is achieved through the use of a pointed tungsten tip in a high vacuum in a strong

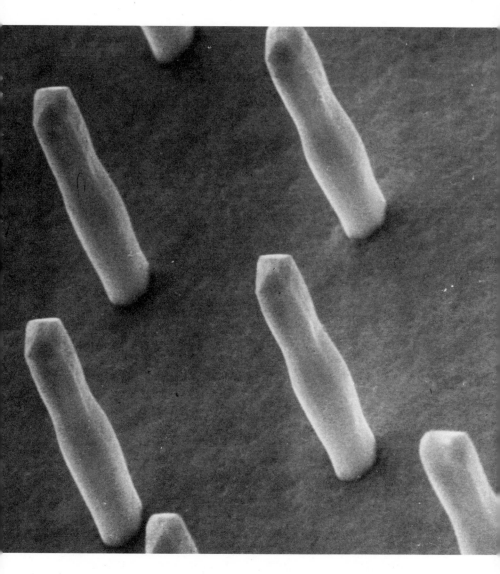

A scanning electron microscope was used to make this highly magnified (18,000 times) picture of a new type of material, called "oxide metal-oxide eutectic composites." This cross-section shows tiny tungsten rods which are about one-thousandths the diameter of a human hair.

electrical field at room temperature. Some of the advantages of the STEM over the TEM are as follows: Simultaneous dark and bright field images are available. Because of point-by-point signal processing, there is no color distortion in and around the image. Also, change in focus or image rotation is possible. Sometimes the STEM is designated as EMMA (electron microscope microprobe analyzer). In this form it can provide microscopic chemical analysis by detecting the spectrum of secondary X rays (X rays that result from atoms of the specimen being struck by electrons emitted from the STEM's tip) and electrons.

Often, another machine, the electron-probe microanalyzer (EPMA), is combined with the SEM. When a solid specimen is struck by a beam of electrons, secondary X rays are generated from the core scattering of the electrons, which yields a continuous spectrum of X rays. Every atom yields a characteristic spectrum of X rays.

Field-emission microscopes (FEMs) are used in metallurgy—the study of metals and their properties. There are two types of field-emission microscopes, both developed by Erwin W. Müller. The first one, developed in 1936, uses the tip of a very sharp negatively charged needle, which is actually the specimen to be observed, in a high vacuum to generate electrons that project a point image on a positively charged fluorescent screen (see fig. 4a and fig. 4b). The FEM, then, is a specialized cathode-ray tube in which the specimen is the cathode. The electron FEM is remarkable in that it can resolve or detect single or small groups of atoms. It also allows scientists to study emission of electrons as a function of surface structure. Organic compounds can also be studied when evaporated onto a clean metal point. The second device, called the field-ion microscope developed in 1950, uses an anode that emits ions.

The ion FEM (called FIM, for field-ion microscope) uses a heat-resistant metal tip and a specimen in a very high vacuum. The tip is charged positively. A gas, such as helium, is introduced and ionized on the tip. The me-

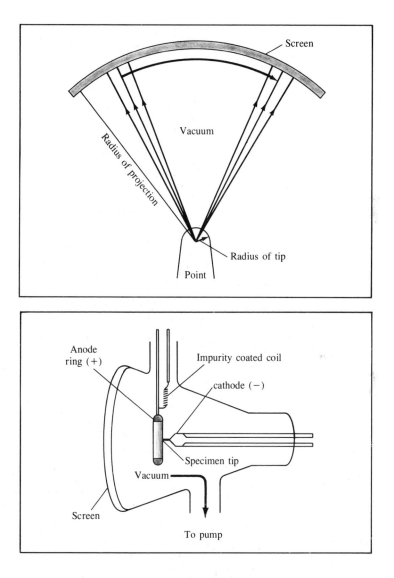

Figure 4a. (above) The principle of point-projection and field-emission microscopes. Figure 4b. (below) A schematic drawing of the electron field-emission microscope. The coil coated with an impurity may be heated to evaporate its atoms onto the point for the purpose of making emission studies.

A technician using an electron field-emission microscope to inspect and image a specimen

ORNL-Photo 5278

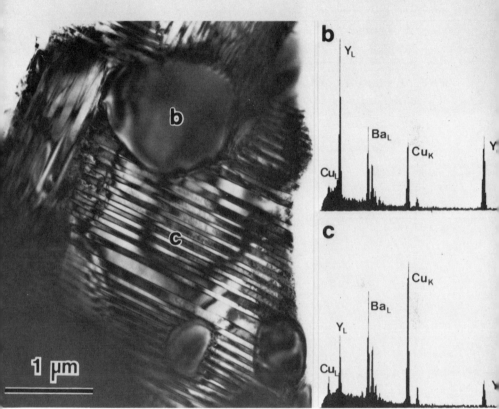

A micrograph made by a field-emission microscope of a high-temperature superconductive material. Part (a) indicates the crystalline structure of the material while (b) and (c) indicate the elemental composition of the material by energy dispersive x-ray analysis.

tallic tip is etched and thinned until it has a radius of only 5 to 100 nm, invisible to the naked eye. Because of the etching, the tip is roughened until its atoms stand out in a series of ridges. Then several thousand volts of electricity are applied to the tip positively; the screen is negatively charged. The tip, cooled by liquid hydrogen and electrically charged, causes atoms of the gas to be attracted to the sharp tip of the specimen. These atoms literally hop along the specimen tip and as they are slowed in their movement, they lose an electron to the specimen. The

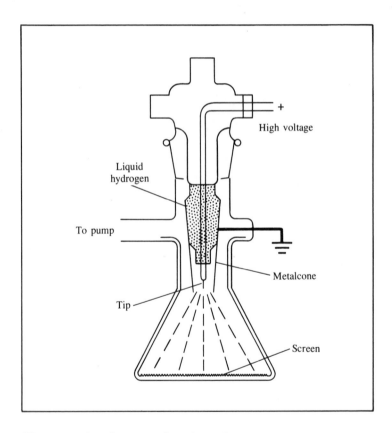

Figure 5. A schematic drawing of a field-ion microscope (FIM).

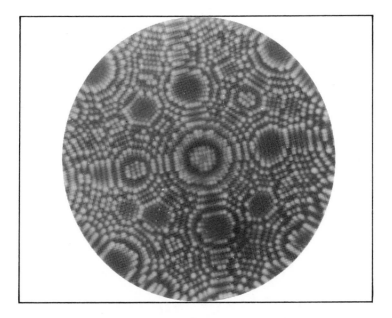

A micrograph done with a field-ion microscope of nickel and molybdenum atoms magnified 5 million times

helium ions then start toward the fluorescent screen, where they release light in a dim pattern. (See fig. 5). The image is photographed using very fast film and lenses, or it may be intensified photoelectronically.

Because there are no lenses in either the FEM or the FIM, depth of field (the thickness of an object in space that is simultaneously in acceptable focus) is quite adequate. The field of view is small because of the small specimen tip. Cleanliness is a must in both the FEM and FIM, as with other electron microscopes.

The primary use of field-emission microscopes is in metallurgy. For example, surface vacancies (missing atoms in the molecules) can be seen by introducing various gases; and slip bands and fractures (weaknesses in the crystalline structure) can be made to appear by varying

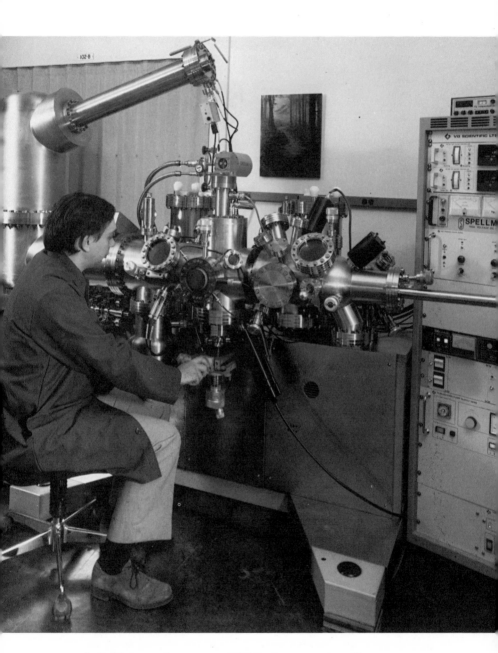

A field-ion microscope (FIM) that can visualize atoms

the voltage and rearrangement of the atoms on the tip during the heating process. Also, the effects of radiation and chemical reactions can be observed on the metal surfaces.

Another type of electron microscope is the proton-scattering microscope. It uses a beam of protons that are accelerated from a gun or ion source. The ion beam is focused onto a metal crystal, such as tungsten or copper. As the protons strike the metal crystal they are scattered, and then the scattered protons strike a fluorescent screen in a distinctive pattern. The patterns then can be analyzed as to the structure of the metal crystals.[7]

X-RAY MICROSCOPY

There are two ways to use the very short wavelength X rays in microscopy. One is to use the X rays themselves to image the specimen. The other is to use almost a reverse process, that is, to get an image from the specimen by the X rays it emits after being struck by electrons.

X rays are of the same nature as visible light; however, they are only about $\frac{1}{1000}$ the wavelength. The rays penetrate the specimen, whether it be a tooth, a part of the body, or an inorganic object, and the X-ray shadow can be recorded as a photograph. Because ordinary X rays have very poor definition, microscopic examination of an X ray is limited. However, the development of point source of X rays, a narrow beam or bundle of almost parallel X rays, allows a closer inspection of specimens exposed to X rays.

The first approach to obtaining a concentrated point source of X rays was to use the objective lens of an electron microscope. Today, commercial electromagnetic lenses are available. The concentrated point X rays, because of their short wavelengths, give high resolving power, and magnification of two hundred times is possible. No vacuum is necessary because X rays travel easily through air.

___

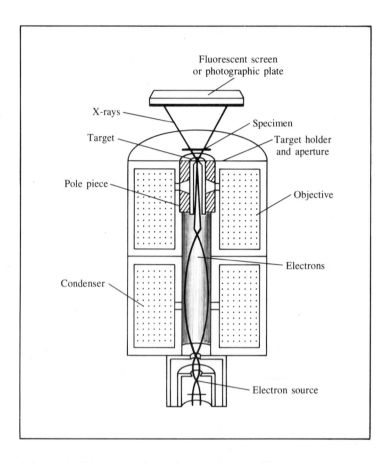

Figure 6. Diagram of a point-projection X-ray microscope.

Specimens can be either organic or inorganic, live or wet. The imaging of these specimens is possible because of X rays' penetrating power. (See fig. 6.)

The electron-probe microanalyzer provides information about the chemical makeup of the specimen being examined. Most other electron microscopes do not. The process is one of examining intensity of the characteristic X rays that are emitted from a specimen when a focused electron beam strikes the specimen. In early models, the electron beam did not move, but today, it scans the specimen. These microscopes are able to get very high resolution, approaching that of TEMs, and will not destroy the specimen. The X-ray image is then focused on a cathode-ray tube—an X-ray microprobe analyzer. This device has turned out to be so valuable that it is now available as an accessory, with an X-ray spectrometer, to existing TEMs as well as combined instruments. The electron-probe microanalyzer is used in metallurgical, biological, and mineralogical work because of its ability to provide chemical information.

A machine that has been used to image polio viruses uses X-ray diffraction. This technique has ordinarily been applied only to crystals, hence the process is often called X-ray crystallography. The use of X-ray diffraction on biological materials had not been too fruitful, as these specimens weakly scatter the X rays, making intensities very difficult to detect.

An accidental discovery in the 1950s at the University of California at Berkeley was made as a researcher there had allowed some polio viruses to crystallize. It was not until much later, though, that technology allowed researchers to image the crystals of polio viruses. As X rays have short wavelengths, around 1.5 Å, they are extremely valuable in discerning individual atoms in a specimen. The problem lay, though, with the appropriate techniques. Simply put, the procedure is to have X rays pass through a slotted device which eliminates stray beams; then the focused beam strikes the crystalline sample. As the X rays pass through the sample, they are scattered in a pattern defined by the structure of the sample. The image is recorded on a photographic film. A computer is used to analyze the image and calculate the positions of the electrons and atoms and then to display the image on a TV screen.

In the case of polio viruses, because they are made of

protein and are quite complex in their structure, millions of measurements are necessary to image them properly. Almost five million measurements were made on eighty-four polio virus crystals before the researchers were finally able to image and describe the structure of the virus. This important research has led to the understanding of the forms of the virus and how it works. It is hoped that this research will help in the fight against viral infections.[8]

ACOUSTIC MICROSCOPES

One of the newer areas of microscopy is that of acoustic microscopes. These acoustic microscopes use electronic signals that, by means of a piezoelectric transducer, are transformed into acoustic waves. (The piezoelectric transducer is a device that converts electromagnetic signals into sound waves and in turn converts sound waves into electromagnetic signals.) These waves are like sound waves in air and waves in water; that is, they are of the multiplying elastic type—as they hit objects new waves are formed. The acoustic waves are of very high frequency, and therefore are ultrasonic and can't be heard. As the projected waves strike the specimen, they are reflected or deflected depending on the density or stiffness of the specimen.

There are two types of acoustic microscopes. One utilizes a scanning laser and is called a scanning laser acoustic microscope (SLAM). The other is a scanning acoustic microscope (SAM) in which the specimen is moved mechanically. The SAM operates through the use of two sapphire crystal lenses immersed in liquid. One lens serves as a condenser of the acoustic beam, while the other serves as the objective lens which allows a sharp focus. (See fig. 7a and fig. 7b.) The SLAM has no lenses and its resolution is limited by the ultrasound's wavelength and the diameter of the moving laser beam.

In the SAM, the acoustic waves, after striking the specimen, are converted by the piezoelectric transducer

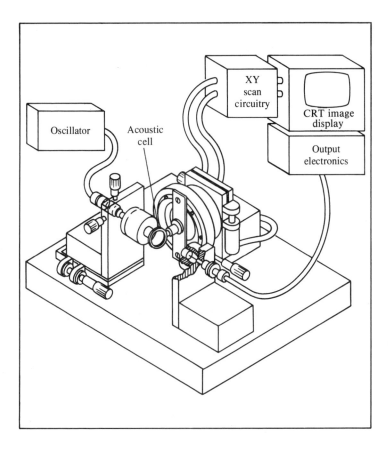

Figure 7a. Diagram of a scanning acoustic microscope (SAM).

into electromagnetic signals which are then imaged on the TV screen. In the SLAM, the acoustical beam modulates the laser beam. The modulated laser beam is received by two photodetectors that give two signals. One signal yields the optical features of the specimen while the other signal yields the acoustic signal from within the specimen. The two signals are displayed on two different TV monitors. These images, for better comparative purposes, may be superimposed.

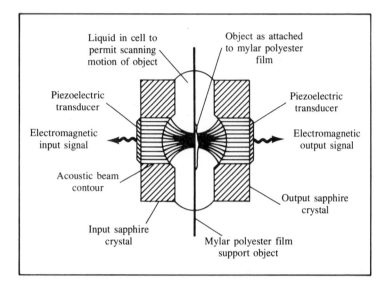

Figure 7b. A schematic drawing of the acoustic cell as used in the SAM.

Acoustic microscopes have been quite valuable in medical research, such as in studies of malignant blood cells, glands, tissues, and bone structure. In studying industrial materials, scientists, using acoustic microscopes, have been able to analyze changes in elasticity of materials on a microscopic scale for the first time. Until recently, because of the high frequencies used, only surface flaws could be detected. However, newer acoustical microscopes, operating at frequencies of up to 100 MHz, can penetrate several inches into specimens ranging in size up to 250-pound (11.3-kg) engine components. At the lower end of their frequency range, the microscopes can image four inches deep into metals and detect flaws 1/100 of an inch wide. The upper limits of the microscope's frequency range can penetrate only a quarter of an inch, but is able to detect flaws 1/1000 of an inch wide.[9]

HIGH-VOLTAGE
ELECTRON MICROSCOPES

High-voltage electron microscopes (HVEMs) differ from conventional electron microscopes in only a few, though important, ways. First, the HVEM is around three stories in height versus the 6 feet (1.8 m) of the conventional one. Second is the cost: up to $3 million for an HVEM versus $200,000 for a conventional one. And third, a conventional electron microscope uses a 100 kilovolt beam while the HVEM uses up to a 1.2 million volt beam. However, the greatest difference is in the penetrating power of the HVEM. It can penetrate a slice of tissue as thick as 1 micron or 10,000 Å as compared with conventional electron microscopes that only pass through specimens less than 2,000 Å thick.

As voltages increase in the electron microscopes, the X rays generated become increasingly hard and penetrating and pose a hazard to the operator. Lead walls or shields are used to keep the X rays confined within the instrument. Besides the shielding, radiation monitors must be placed in various parts of the microscope room to make sure that the operator is not being exposed to X rays at unacceptable levels. If X rays exceed proper levels, alarms sound, alerting the operator and others to shut down the machine and evacuate the area.

The superior penetrating power of HVEMs makes it possible to examine the network of structures within cells. One of the important contributions of HVEMs was in the investigation of the structural arrangement of a cell's cytoplasm. At one time cell cytoplasm was thought to be a disorganized grouping of matter; then it was found to be a solid gel studded with intracellular structures called organelles, much like Jell-O with fruit. HVEMs revealed details of these structures. HVEMs have also been used in the investigation of nerve cells and how they function, structural changes in chromosomes during cell division, and gene activity.

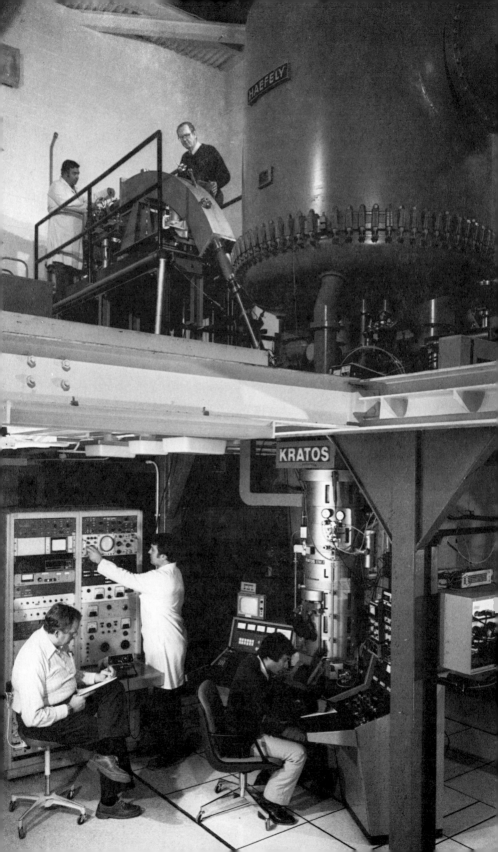

Two sets of the same images produced by an HVEM may be viewed by using special glasses to produce a stereo or three-dimensional effect to get a depth dimension of biological specimens. However, even better and more startling three-dimensional images can be produced from HVEMs by the use of computer analysis of the images. A series of images of a single specimen is taken from a variety of angles. The information from the images is then processed by a computer to generate a three-dimensional view on a display screen. The computer can manipulate the image on the screen in several ways, such as showing the specimen from a certain angle or imaging a slice of the specimen. Also, colors can be added to the image to differentiate and distinguish various structures.[10]

Recently, intermediate-voltage electron microscopes (IVEMs), electron microscopes that use electron beams of 300 to 400 kilovolts, have been introduced. Because of their much smaller size and comparatively low cost, about $1 million each, it was first thought that these microscopes might replace HVEMs. Also, some scientists believe that the images produced by IVEMs could approach those produced by HVEMs. However, it seems that the IVEMs will not replace the HVEMs but will serve as feeders to HVEMs for projects where the higher voltage machines are needed; these million-volt machines will continue to allow new discoveries and investigations, especially in the areas of neurobiology and chromosome structure analysis.

A high-voltage electron microscope (HVEM) that can magnify up to 1 million times, enabling scientists to observe radiation damage as it occurs at the molecular level

A scanning-tunneling electron microscope (STM) which allows exploration of specimen surfaces at atomic resolutions

A silicon surface as pictured by a scanning-tunneling electron microscope. The contour rings are separated by only ⅙ Å.

THE SCANNING-TUNNELING MICROSCOPE

In 1981, scientists at the IBM Research Laboratory developed a powerful new version of an electron microscope, the scanning-tunneling microscope (STM), through which the observer could see individual atoms in a solid surface. With today's improved STM, the observer is not only able to see atoms, but to identify their chemical species as well. The microscopes can work in a variety of environments ranging from a vacuum to liquids and at a wide range of temperatures.

The instruments work because of the quantum mechanical effect called tunneling. When two electrodes are separated from one another by a vacuum or insulating material, no current will flow between them until the voltage is high enough to burn out the insulation or to spark. However, it was conceptualized in quantum mechanics that long before this event occurred, if the gap were narrow enough between the two electrodes, one or two Å, tunneling electric current would cross through the barrier.

The STM is constructed so that one electrode is a sharply shaped probe; the surface of the specimen to be examined serves as the other electrode. The probe's tip scans the specimen's surface at a distance of a few atomic diameters. Then a tunneling electric current flows between the surface and the tip, but the surface and the tip never touch. Surface roughness of the specimen will cause the distance between the tip and the surface to vary, causing changes in the current. These differences in current allow the STM to accurately image the surface.

Besides the remarkable pictures available from the STM, it has been extremely helpful in a number of different kinds of investigations. It has been used with wet specimens to examine viruses, to examine the electronic surfaces of conductors, and to study molecular vibrations. By using parallel scans, three-dimensional images are available on the atomic level.

The newest STM, except for the vacuum chamber, can fit into a person's hand and is capable of a vertical resolution of 0.1 Å and a lateral resolution of 2 Å, using tips of only a few atoms wide.

Amazingly, in 1986, for inventions almost one-half century apart, the Royal Academy of Science split the Nobel Prize for Physics between Ernst Ruska of West Berlin and Gerd Binnig and Heinrich Rohrer of Zurich, Switzerland. Ruska received his award for "his fundamental work in electron optics and for the design of the first electron microscope." Binnig and Rohrer of the IBM Research Laboratory received their award "for design of the Scanning Tunneling Microscope." These awards highlight the remarkable progress that has been made in electron microscopy. Further, the awarding of the Nobel prize for these two inventions brought into focus the research and advancements made possible by microscopes that do not use light.[11]

The variety of nonlight microscopes that have appeared since Ruska's invention have been responsible for many amazing discoveries and applications. Of course, the major contribution has been that these instruments allow scientists, researchers, and engineers to see minute objects with greater detail than ever before. As a result, applications of these machines are almost unlimited.

One of the most amazing discoveries came in 1951 when Erwin W. Müller first imaged the atoms of iridium. In 1975, Albert Crewe and his coworkers at the University of Chicago were able to take motion pictures of uranium atoms in motion. In the 1970s, the viruses causing hepatitis were first viewed through the electron microscope.

Current applications of these machines range over a variety of industrial and research settings. Commercial EMs are used in the metallurgy industries and for research to study the atomic structure of metals, to analyze the crystalline structures of metals, and to analyze these structures for fractures and flaws. Metals and materials such as rubber and plastics can be examined under stress and in corrosive and degenerative situations, too. The makeup of fibrous materials, such as cotton and wood pulp, can be examined, as well as the impact of various coatings, as on paper, for effect and strength. Electron microscopes are widely used in the electronics industry in examining semiconductors and microcircuits to understand how they work and how they behave under stress and their behavior under the onset of superconductivity. Electron microscopes are now used to examine metals and machine parts for surface and interior flaws. Biologists are using these machines to investigate such things as the composition of soil and the anatomy of cells and how cells function, and in research on genetic structures. Medical researchers use the machines to see inside the human body—the structure and functioning of cells, the brain and nervous system, the effects of disease on the body, and how bacteria and viruses work.

The development of electron microscopes and similar imaging machines is fairly recent, and what we have learned from them has advanced science by quantum leaps. It is apparent, however, that even though we have come far, there are many more discoveries yet to be made of the world invisible to our eyes.

THREE

A CLOSER VIEW OF OUR BODIES

In 1895, in the course of experimenting with a Crookes tube, William Konrad Roentgen (1845–1923) discovered X rays. Although other scientists had studied cathode tubes (of which the Crookes tube was an early type) and the rays these tubes emitted, Roentgen was the first to discover that these rays, resulting from electrons striking the metal targets, would emit light, or fluoresce, when striking a surface coated with barium platinocyanide. Further, he found that these surfaces would fluoresce even when shielded from the visible and ultraviolet light emitted by the cathode tube. He called them X rays because of their unknown nature.

In experimenting with X rays, it was found that when an X-ray beam passes through an object, the object itself will become a source of secondary X rays, and because of this process a portion of the beam is absorbed. Also, X rays travel in straight lines, as Roentgen discovered, and they affect photographic film. Further, it was discovered that X rays' penetrating ability increases with increasing energy of incidental electrons and that the intensity of the X-ray beam is proportional to the number of electrons per second striking the target.

X rays, like other forms of energy, have characteristics of both waves and particles. X rays are much like light waves, though their wavelengths are much shorter than visible or ultraviolet light wavelengths. According to the quantum theory, X rays also consist of small distinct packets of energy known as quanta, or photons.

X rays may be detected in two major ways. The first is through the ability of X rays to cause photochemical changes on film or a photographic emulsion. The other is that X rays can produce fluorescence or ionization in a variety of substances. A variety of devices called electronic detectors, which range from scintillation counters to ionization chambers, detect X rays nonphotographically. These machines act like counting devices since a signal is produced by each absorbed photon, and therefore, the number of photons can be determined. These machines can detect the amount of radiation at different wavelengths.

Today there are many applications for X rays. In industry X rays are used to detect hidden flaws in castings and other materials and to determine the thickness of materials by measuring the absorption in a sample. However, in medicine, the three most important uses of X rays are their ability to penetrate the human body, their imaging effects on photographic film after they penetrate the body, and their ability to treat diseases, such as cancer. When Roentgen first imaged his hand using X rays, it was the beginning of a new epoch in medicine and the founding of roentgenology, the science of imaging the body and using these recorded photographic images for diagnosis.

Later, the term *radiology* supplanted the term *roentgenology*, and today the term *imaging* is used because it covers a spectrum of techniques whereby energy is used to generate visual images of an object.[12]

COMPUTER TOMOGRAPHY

As useful as the X ray is, it often has serious shortcomings as a medical tool. The most obvious one, of course, is that the X ray itself can be a danger to the patient. There is a limit to the amount of radiation an individual can be exposed to without adverse effects. Also, the X ray itself is limited in the amount of detail it can image even with the advent of the modern innovations of image intensification and geometric tomography, that is, imaging of selected planes of the body.

In 1972, Godfrey Hounsfield and a team of experts at the British Institute of Radiology developed the first clinically useful computerized tomography (CT) scanner, an event as important as the discovery of X rays by Roentgen. Hounsfield and his colleagues had worked several years in great secrecy to develop the CT scanner. At first, a lathe bed (a machine in which the work is held and rotated while being shaped by a tool) was used as the gantry (the movable frame that holds the X-ray tube, the detector, and electronics for the machine), and the isotope americium as the energy source. Americium was soon replaced with an X-ray tube, reducing the exposure time from nine days to nine hours. Using brain tissue and pig abdomens for specimens, the British team was able to distinguish between white and gray matter in brains, as well as to discern easily muscle, fat, and other body tissue. Today, scan time has been reduced to twenty seconds or less, depending on the type of machine and the scan necessary.

CT is known by a variety of names—computed axial tomography (CAT), computer-aided tomography (CAT), computed transmission tomography (CTT), as well as several other terms. However, they all operate using the same principles. Using CTs, the observer can see the specific part of the body to be examined without the obstruction of overlaying structures. For example, the liver can be imaged, without the rib cage, muscles, skin, etc., showing. Conventional tomography does not meet the needs of sharp imaging and contrast.

Computerized tomography, however, eliminates the poor images often obtained from conventional tomography through a variety of means. CTs use special image detectors, multiple X-ray transmission readings, highly collimated (accurate and parallel) X-ray beams, and a computer for the computation of the complex mathematics used to reconstruct a cross-sectional image. In essence, CT is a digital imaging technique that uses X rays to scan a patient, then measures the data from many points in space and converts the X-ray and intensity values into electrical signals. These signals, analog data, are then given a numerical value that is converted to digital data. The digital data are then processed by the computer, which in turn displays the image. Imagine that you placed a leg of lamb in a CT scanner to image it. What you could see is an image of that leg, layer by layer, down to the center of the bone. You could see things not evident to the human eye on a conventional X ray and you could see air pockets, if any.

A CT scanning system (fig. 8) is usually made up of five major units: (1) the gantry, (2) X-ray source, (3) the computers, (4) console and image display, and (5) image storage and production devices.

The gantry is the movable frame of the CT system in which the X-ray production system is housed. It has a large opening (aperture) for the patient or specimen to pass back and forth while lying on the table to be scanned. The patient may be scanned in a variety of positions; however, the body must be positioned or aligned centrally and either white lights or low-powered lasers which shine

Sue Holloway, a technician, is at the control console of an emission computerized axial tomography scanner. Next to the scanner is Dr. James Crook, head of the Clinical Nuclear Medicine Program at Oak Ridge Associated Universities.

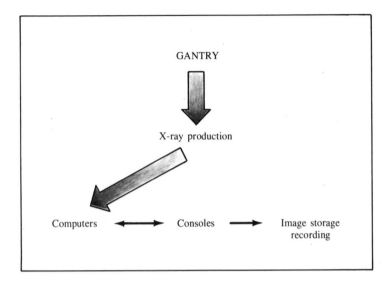

Figure 8. Diagram of the five major components of a CT system.

on the patient are used to position the body and indicate if the patient is accurately positioned for the best image. The X-ray production unit consists of either a stationary or a rotating tube. The number and placement of detectors depends on which generation of machine it is.

Depending on the type of CT scanner, computer configuration varies (see fig. 9). However, the computer must have a large enough capacity to store and process the massive amount of data involved in CT. The operating consoles, which control the computer, are of three main types: (1) the operating console where the operator controls the overall system, (2) the reporting console where the medical personnel can view the image and also generate reports, and (3) an independent viewing reporting console that has its own central processing unit and disk drive that may or may not be linked to the main computer processing unit.

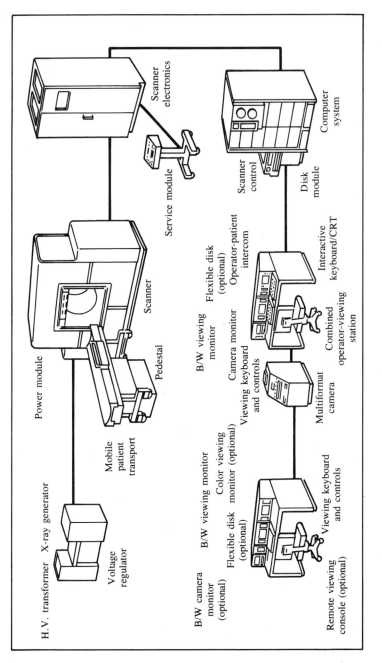

Figure 9. The functional relationship of the components of a CT scanner.

The image is displayed on one or more of the console's TV screens. The image, in various shades of gray, can be manipulated in a variety of ways by the operator for contrast and density, a process called windowing. For example, the same picture, through the windowing process, can be made to emphasize the bone, tissue, or water of the area scanned.

Scans may be recorded, stored, and retrieved in several ways. The computer may record and store the information on magnetic tapes or floppy disks. Hard copies of images can be obtained by the use of Polaroid film, or silver dry paper, printouts of CT numbers, or 35mm slides using a multiformat camera.

As good as CTs are in imaging the human body, there are often circumstances which will cause artifact structures or false images not naturally appearing in the tissues to be observed. These artifacts can appear as streaks, rings, shading, cupping, capping, or artificial shading in the center of the scan field of view. Streaks may appear on the image as a result of patient movement. Multiple dental fillings, a metal plate in the patient, and a zipper on an article of clothing are examples of items that may also cause streaking. Other false images may occur because of machine or operator error. These are reasons why it is imperative that a quality assurance program be carried out on a regular basis. For example, a water-filled phantom (a test object, body shaped, that mimics body tissue) with known CT numbers should be scanned daily. Other tests for calibrations should be carried out on a weekly basis. Also, it is very important that the radiation dose from the scanner be checked every few weeks for protection of the patient.

The CT, in its short history, has greatly improved many areas of medical diagnosis. It has made it possible for physicians to perform operations that they might not have been able to perform a few years ago. It is now widely used to pinpoint malignant tumors. With the CT's ability to project three-dimensional images of humans, it is playing an important role in reconstructive surgery. One scanner, known as a dynamic spatial reconstructor, gives three-dimensional images coupled with high-speed imagery. The projection of three-dimensional pictures of the heart as it beats is just one of its uses.

VARIETIES OF CTS

At present, there are four generations of CTs. First-generation scanners use a single pencil-beam X ray with a few detectors (fig. 10a). In this system a 180° radius of the patient was scanned in 1° increments until the area to be scanned was completed. Total scan time involved is four to five minutes. Third-generation CTs use a fan beam with multiple detectors (fig. 10b). The X ray and the detectors move in tandem around the patient and are much

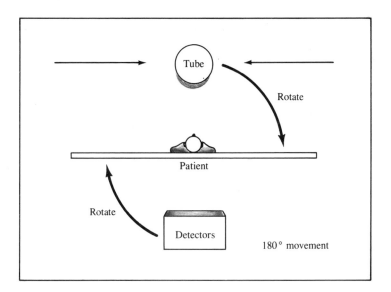

Figure 10a. First-generation scanners use a single pencil-beam X ray. A 180° radius of the patient is scanned in 1° increments.

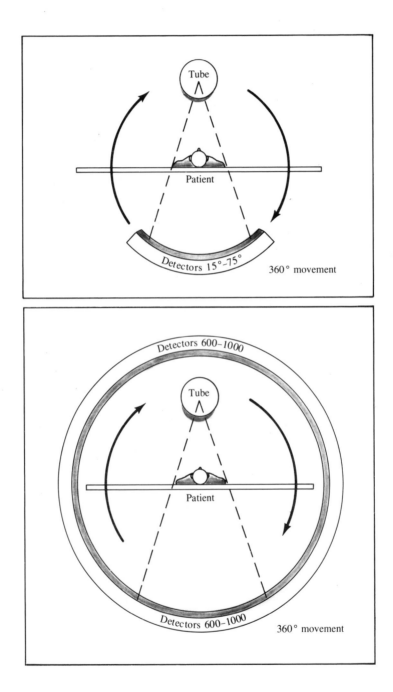

faster than earlier-generation CTs. Fourth-generation scanners differ from the first three generations in that the X ray is a wide fan beam with the 600 to 2,000 stationary detectors forming a circle around the patient (fig. 10c). Scan time is two to twenty seconds. In one model of a fourth-generation scanner, the detectors closest to the X-ray tube move, so that the rays will hit the detectors that are further away.

Detectors are an integral part of the CT. They capture the transmitted X rays, convert them to electrical signals, and pass them on to the data acquisition system for conversion to digital form.

There are two types of detectors. The first is the scintillation type, which consists of a scintillation crystal and a photomultiplier tube. The crystal most commonly used is sodium iodide. The crystal converts X rays into light photons proportionate to the energy of the X rays it receives, and then the photomultiplier tube converts these into electrical signals.

The other type of detector is based on gas ionization. The detector is filled with a pressurized gas like xenon. As the X rays hit the detector, the gas is ionized and then an electrical signal is produced.

Both types of detectors have advantages and disadvantages. Crystal detectors using sodium iodide have high efficiency as compared with those using other crystals, but they exhibit afterglow. If sodium iodide is combined with

Figure 10b. (above) Third-generation scanners use a fan beam with multiple detectors. Figure 10c. (below) Fourth-generation scanners have a wide fan beam with 600 to 2,000 detectors.

another compound to reduce afterglow, sensitivity is reduced. Gas-ionization detectors using xenon do not exhibit afterglow, but they do exhibit lower absorption than crystal detectors. It seems, then, that the two types of detectors have about the same efficiency. However, the crystal detectors' range is more limited than that of gas-ionization detectors.

The imaging process using a CT is very different from that of a conventional X ray. Rather than obtaining an image through the process of X rays passing through a patient and the penetrating X rays being received on photographic film, a very technical mathematical process is used. Initially, two measurements are made. For the first, as the beam leaves the X-ray tube, its intensity is measured by the reference detector. The second measurement is taken by the detector below the patient, which registers the intensity of the transmitted photons. Then by dividing the intensity of the X rays at their source by the intensity of the X rays at the detector and then multiplying by a logarithm (the exponent of that power to which a fixed number must be raised in order to produce a given number), the relative transmission values are calculated. These values are in turn used to calculate CT numbers.

CT numbers are calculated by using the following formula:

$$\text{CT Number} = \frac{\text{tissue} - \text{water}}{\text{water}} \times C$$

(tissue and water being assigned coefficients or weights). That is, C being the CT manufacturer's scaling or contrast factor (usually 500 to 1,000). Most manufacturers now use the Hounsfield scale for C, which extends from $+1,000$ for bone through o for water to $-1,000$ for air. Once the CT numbers are computed, they are then fed into a computer to reconstruct the image. A printout of numbers can then be generated, but it is often hard to interpret directly. Therefore, an image can be displayed on a TV screen using these numbers as a data base. The generated data are converted from digital data to analog data and then can be displayed in varying shades of gray. The TV-screen matrix is made up of pixels, and these pixels are illuminated in various shades and represent the CT number computed for a specific volume of tissue, which is called a voxel.

Although image enhancement would seem a natural extension of CT technology it actually stemmed from work done in the field of astronomy. Because astronomers are not always able to see their objects clearly, work done by NASA and others led to the digital enhancement of images by using a computer. You probably have seen this many times in news coverage of American spaceflights, and most recently, the pictures of Halley's comet that were digitally enhanced by computers.[13]

CHARTING BLOOD FLOW

Using X rays and computers, digital subtraction angiography (DSA) is one of these new techniques being used in medicine. DSA is used for charting the flow of blood in veins and arteries, especially in and around the heart. First, a conventional X ray is taken of the heart, for example, and stored in the computer. Then an opaque iodine dye is injected into the blood stream for contrast and a second X ray is taken. The information from the two X rays is converted from analog data to digital data and then processed by the computer. The computer then digitally subtracts one image from the other, giving a sharp image of the blood flow and an indication of whether any blood vessels or arteries are clogged or not working properly.

If the surgeon sees a blockage in the blood supply to the heart, there are two courses of action. One is to surgically open the chest and bypass the blocked blood vessel, replacing it with one usually taken from the leg. This is called heart bypass surgery. The other approach is a procedure called coronary angioplasty. Using the DSA technique, a surgeon can thread a catheter into a coronary artery by way of a blood vessel in the arm or leg. Again, a contrast agent is used to provide a clear image of the blockage, and then a second smaller catheter is inserted into the first one and positioned next to the blockage. Then a balloon is inflated inside the blood vessel until it compresses the materials causing the blockage, allowing normal blood flow to resume. The advantage of this technique is that it is cheaper and much less hazardous than open-heart surgery. This safer operation has resulted from using the computer in combination with X rays.

Since the development and application of CTs, medical imaging has undergone a dramatic upheaval. New imaging machines have been developed by researchers and made commercially available at an ever-quickening pace. It is not unusual to see articles in newspapers and magazines describing how these new machines work and how they save lives. Such machines are called PETs, SPECTs, and NMRs. Even a best-selling book, *A Machine Called Indomitable* by Sonny Kleinfield, was written about the visionary scientist who developed the NMR and his fight to uphold his patent.

POSITRON EMISSION TOMOGRAPHY

In the 1970s, positron emission tomography (PET) was introduced. Because this imaging machine is quite expensive, there are only a dozen or so in the United States today. Not only is the machine expensive, but it requires the use of a cyclotron, a kind of atom smasher, to make radioisotopes. A common substance, like sugar, is made radioactive with a radioisotope that has a short half-life. This means that the radioisotope loses half of its radioactivity in a few minutes to a few hours.

The patient is placed on a table that slides into the center hole of a large, metallic, doughnut-shaped machine. After being injected with the radioactive solution, the patient is centered and placed in the machine appropriately, depending on the part of the body to be examined. As the radioactive solution flows through the body's blood stream, it emits positrons which collide with electrons in the body. As they collide, they destroy each other and emit energy in the form of two gamma rays.

The resulting gamma rays then shoot out of the patient in opposite directions and strike a ring of crystals in the ring of detectors in the machine. When the crystals are struck by the gamma rays, they emit light. This information is then forwarded to a computer that, in turn, plots the source and location of the rays. The millions of bits of information emitted from the scanning procedures are converted into digital data. The computer then generates an image on a cathode-ray tube. For example, in cases where the heart is being examined, the computer can show on the screen two separate images of the heart and the blood flow: at rest and under stress. These machines have also become extremely useful in studying the brain, especially its action and reaction and how it is affected by disease. Until PET came along, diagnosis of such afflictions as Alzheimer's disease and other forms of dementia could only be confirmed by autopsy after the patient's death. Though PET machines are expensive, they are extraordinary in their ability to analyze anatomy, as well as chemical and physical processes of the body. Through the use of PET, scientists have found that patients suffering from Alzheimer's disease show a lessened blood flow in parts of the brain.

To counter the high costs of building and maintaining PET machines, a new approach has been developed: single photon emission computer tomography (SPECT), also known as single photon emission tomography (SPET).

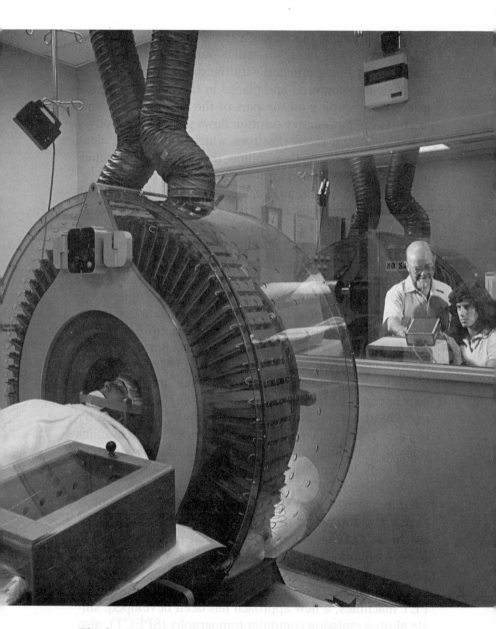

The brain of the patient is being examined by
a positron emission tomography scanner (PET).

The output of the PET scanner shows glucose metabolism in the brain as the patient is given various tasks, such as reading or listening.

Although the components of SPECT are really not new (many of the devices have been used in hospitals since the 1960s), the technique is new. SPECT scanners cost about 10 percent of the cost of a PET machine, from $60,000 to $250,000 compared with $1.6 to $2 million for a typical PET. Also, the cost of operation is less and, with a breakthrough in 1983, the need for a cyclotron close at hand was alleviated. The breakthrough was the development of a new low-cost amphetamine-like compound that could be attached to radioactive iodine. Since the brain is protected by tissues that prevent penetration of most chemicals, this compound could penetrate the brain. Once injected into the bloodstream, it made it possible to image the brain.

Patients being imaged by SPECT are first injected with this new low-cost radioactive tracer. They are then placed in the SPECT machine. The radioactive emissions are recorded by a special camera or cameras and the information is fed into a computer. As with several other imaging devices, the computer analyzes the data and then the computer creates an image on a cathode-ray tube. Like CTs, pictures of different angles of the body are taken. It can produce cross-section images of the patient's body or organs. Though SPECT images are not as clearly defined as PET images, their lower cost allows widespread clinical application for screening such disorders as Alzheimer's disease.

Both PET and SPECT are extremely powerful imaging machines. In fact, often the patient's eyes and ears have to be covered because a bright light or loud noise will cause the portions of the brain that control seeing or hearing to "light up." These machines literally probe the way the mind works.[14]

FOUR

EXPANDING MEDICAL IMAGING

MAGNETIC RESONANCE

One of the most intriguing machines is one that uses nuclear magnetic resonance (NMR) or magnetic resonance imaging (MRI). This new discovery is sometimes hailed as being as great a diagnostic tool as the X ray. The underlying principle of MRI is that when the human body is subjected to a powerful magnetic field and then radio waves, the hydrogen atoms of water in the body will be affected, enabling the MRI to image the body (fig. 11).

MRI has been controversial—not only in its application but also in the subsequent court cases filed over patent infringement by Dr. Raymond Damadion, who built a prototype MRI machine he called Indomitable. Regardless of the controversy, experimenting with the prototype

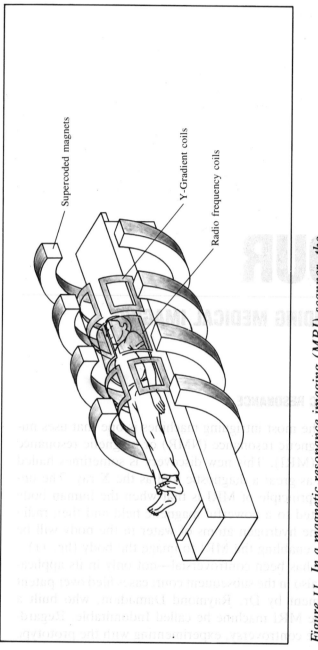

Figure 11. In a magnetic resonance imaging (MRI) scanner, the patient is surrounded by supercooled electromagnets that create a magnetic field 60,000 times as strong as that of the earth.

MRI was often dangerous because no one really knew what powerful magnetic fields would do to the human body. It was thought by some that placing a human head in such a machine would completely erase the human's memory.[15]

Since 1980, when the first commercial MRI was introduced, the use of MRI has expanded greatly. Today, over fifteen companies are building MRI machines and some 500 machines are in use in the United States.

MRI machines are large, heavy, and costly. In many cases, the floor of the room in which the machine is housed must be strengthened to support the weight of the machine. In addition, the room must be totally shielded from external radio waves. The cost of the machine and shielding can often reach $2.75 million.

The machine is cylindrical in shape, with a hollow center where the patient reclines. Surrounding the center are either permanent magnets or superconducting electromagnets cooled with liquid helium. The magnetic field, depending upon the manufacturer, can range from 60 to 300 kilogauss. The machine also has radio frequency coils and y-gradient and x-gradient coils to build up a two-dimensional picture.

When the machine is turned on, the generated strong magnetic field causes the protons, the nuclei of the hydrogen atoms, to change position. The nuclei continuously spin, but in the absence of a strong magnetic field they point in random directions. When they are affected by the strong magnetic field of the MRI magnets, the protons align themselves in the direction of the magnet's poles. Their rate of wobble increases as the magnetic field is increased. At a precise moment, a radio pulse timed to the proton's wobbling is given, causing the protons to fall out of alignment. In a few thousandths of a second, the protons spring back to their original positions and at the same time broadcast a faint radio signal. This procedure repeats itself, sometimes hundreds of times in three dif-

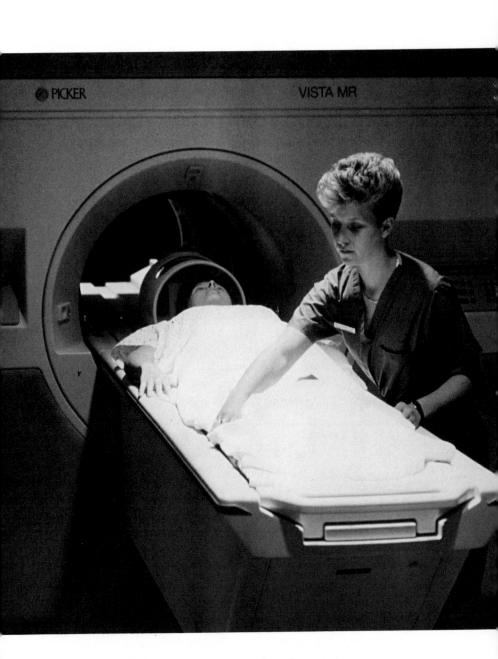

A technologist prepares a patient for a scan by a magnetic resonance imager (EMRI).

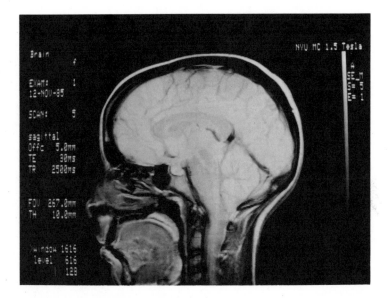

A scan of the human brain, using magnetic resonance imaging.

ferent directions, and the information obtained is fed to the computer as a voxel, a spot on the screen. The voxel is assigned brightness, depending upon the number of protons in the specific spot and the magnetic properties of the tissue. A collection of these voxels form the image of the body being examined.

The computer is very important in MRI because it translates the digital data through the use of complicated programming to make the image. What is obtained is an image of the specific area scanned reflecting the density of the hydrogen atoms and their interaction with the other tissues in a cross-section of the body. Because hydrogen is a component of water, distinctions can be made of the various tissues. Hydrogen was the element of choice because of its abundance in the human body and its magnetic qualities. However, scientists are already investigating using MRI techniques on other body elements to provide early warning of impending strokes or heart attacks. Already MRI has been used to provide noninvasive angiography, imaging without surgery, and to investigate noninvasively how the biochemical laws of energy operate in organs and tissues. Most recently, MRI scans have been made using metallic contrast agents. For example, scientists are using a biodegradable, iron-based compound to detect cancers of the liver. It would seem that MRI images may be much more useful in the future than today, and that having a yearly body scan by MRI may become a preventive health tool because it is noninvasive and nonradioactive.[16]

ULTRASOUND

Of all the medical imaging machines available to scientists and medical personnel, the simplest and least expensive imaging technique is that of ultrasound scans or sonography. Sonography is an outgrowth of sonar, an apparatus used by the military during World War II to track, find, and destroy submarines. Today's sonographic techniques are computer-based, as are so many other imaging techniques. A transducer, or transmitter-receiver, is made up of a piezoelectric crystal that converts electrical pulses into vibrations that can penetrate the body. The generated sound waves are aimed at specific organs or parts of the body and are then reflected back to the crystal, which in turn converts them back into electrical signals. The time delay of the returned signals then allows the computer to image the target's shape, size, and texture on a video screen. Since the procedure is a relatively simple one, the medical personnel can get almost instant image feedback.

A special application of sonography is that of examining fetuses in pregnant women. X rays and other invasive techniques can be extremely hazardous to an unborn child—X rays can cause birth defects. Ultrasound im-

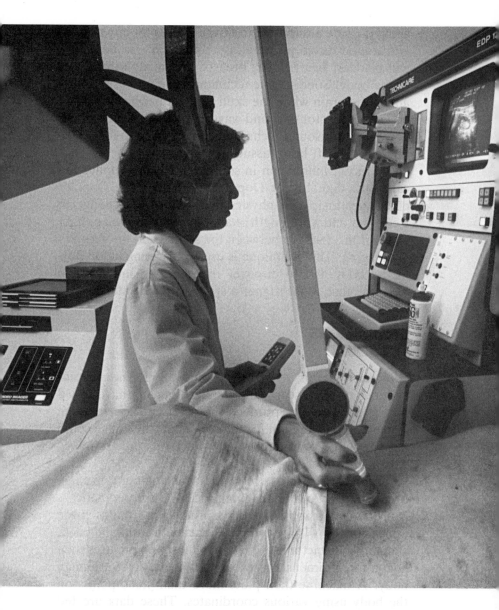

The patient's kidney is being imaged by ultrasound. The screen shows the image of the kidney for inspection by medical personnel.

aging is a safe alternative to image a fetus for any reason. Ultrasound techniques are also suitable for scanning the gall bladder, heart, liver, breasts, and many other parts of the body. Sonographic techniques can't be used to examine the brain while the skull is intact because the skull bone is a reflector of sound waves. Once the skull is open, however, ultrasound techniques can be used to locate tumors in the soft brain tissues.

A recent innovation in sonography is the application called the digital color Doppler technique. The Doppler effect, a principle of physics, is the apparent change in frequency and wavelength of a succession of sound or light waves if the distance between the source and the receiver is changing. This technique is used in charting blood flow in the body and to discover irregularities and possible blockage that could trigger a stroke or heart attack.

OTHER IMAGING TECHNIQUES

As we have seen, most of the innovations and new inventions of microscopy and medical imaging have relied on the computer to produce the actual image. In some instances, if it were not for the computer, the image could probably not be produced, or a much less precise image would be available.

In the case of biostereomatics, the computer is again a valuable part of the imaging process. Biostereomatics is a process of mapping or measuring living things three dimensionally. Using stereo cameras both front and back, simultaneous pictures are taken. The stereo pictures then give a three-dimensional view of, for example, a human body. A machine then plots more than 5,000 points on the body using various coordinates. These data are fed into a computer, which in turn can image the data in almost any configuration wanted. It can isolate various parts of the body and view them from any angle.

The applications of this procedure ranges from determining body volume lost by astronauts after long periods in space, design of body protectors such as helmets, design of artificial limbs, and detection of spinal deformities like scoliosis in children.

Microwaves, radar, and infrared techniques are other methods of imaging that are being investigated to determine their suitability in the diagnosis of disease, detection of abnormalities of the body, and investigation of organs, blood flow, and the like. In many ways these techniques are in their infancy and may never prove to be more valuable than current imaging techniques available today. However, there is considerable research going on in these areas and a major breakthrough in their use may come at any time.

You probably know about microwaves from the microwave oven found in many kitchens and restaurants. These devices heat food quickly by exciting the molecules in a food, causing it to grow hot and literally "cook" itself without generating much heat into the surrounding area.

Scientists use microwaves in the same way but to thaw frozen samples. Microwaves have been used to measure the size of muscle, kidney, brain, fat, and tumors in animals, and skin and surface lesions in humans. Also, microwaves have been used extensively to measure the dielectric (nonconductive) properties of body organs and the relationship of dielectric properties of tissues and blood flow. A further use of microwaves has been to determine both the intensity and distribution of doses of medicine in body dosimetry studies—measurement of doses.

An interesting application of medical imaging is that of using the electrical impedance, or the electrical resistant characteristics of the human body, to image body structures noninvasively. This technique is based on the fact that voltages applied to different areas of the body cause it to conduct different amounts of current. Applying this technique to the three planes of the body could give a three-dimensional view of the body. It is well known that body conductivity varies in differing regions of the body. For example, blood is the most conductive, whereas the lungs and bones are the least conductive. Though the technique of impedance looks promising, data from humans have not been used in reconstructing images. Most experiments have been done using objects to simulate human parts of the body. There have been a few experiments using a human forearm that used a circle of electrodes to measure the impedance by measuring the potential difference between the adjacent pairs of electrodes. Images did show the bone and fat in the forearm with limited resolution. It seems clear at this point that the technique of electrical impedance for imaging may be a definite possibility in the future, but many more investigations and extremely effective computers and methods of analysis are needed.

Radar, as a measurement technique, has long been used to gather information from great distances. Scientists have wondered whether radar may have applications in biological and/or human imaging as well. There is some work being done in this field that may be fruitful in the future, but at present it seems doubtful that there is any major important application for radar to human imaging.

Today's physicians and surgeons have access to a multitude of diagnostic tools. Besides conventional X rays, the doctor may use CT scans, PET scans, MRI scans, or sonograms. It is not uncommon for a surgeon in an operating room to use several of these images before and during surgery as guides.

Since the 1950s, optical surgical microscopes have aided the surgeon to see, cut, and suture many parts of the body. Surgical microscopes today allow magnification of up to forty times to allow microsurgery to be performed on eyes, nerves, ducts, ureters, and coronary arteries. The surgeon is aided even further through the use of fiber optics—flexible fiber-filled tubes that can transmit light to enable the doctor to look into the orifices of the body, or, where small incisions have been made, to inspect damage to bone, cartilage, or muscle.

For today's medical practitioner, the view of our bodies is becoming increasingly clearer every day through the use of these new imaging machines. These machines have made it possible for physicians to discover diseases long before they would become apparent as tumors or bodily defects. As a result of these new machines, even more amazing discoveries may come in the future. For example, an oncoming disease could be identified by certain chemical changes in the body, or cloned antibodies, with magnetically traceable elements, could be used to discover cancerous tumors not otherwise identifiable at the time.[17]

FIVE

EYES ON SPACE

Probably no one knows who really discovered the telescope, as glass was made in ancient Egypt as early as 3500 B.C., and crude glass lenses date as far back as 2000 B.C. We do know that the ancient Sumerians, Greeks, and Romans studied the heavens and devised systems for measuring the movements of the planets. In 1580, the Danish astronomer Tycho Brahe (1546–1601) established the first astronomical laboratory to study the heavens. Later, his German assistant, Johannes Kepler, continued his work and in 1609 published his account of the elliptical orbits of the planets.

About the same time that Kepler was publishing his work about the course of the planets, the Dutchman Hans Lippershey (1587–1619) devised an optical telescope. In all probability, Lippershey did not "invent" the telescope, but he should be credited with making the instrument known to the world by offering it to the Dutch government as a tool of war. The telescope enabled the Dutch to spot approaching ships long before those ships were aware of the position of the Dutch ships.

Lippershey's telescope was of the refractory type. Refracting telescopes are those that bend light through the use of an objective lens and an eyepiece.

The Italian Galileo Galilei (1564–1642), who heard of Lippershey's invention—at least according to the story Galileo told—built his own telescope in a day. At first, he, too, envisioned it as a tool of war and demonstrated it to the leaders of Venice as a way of detecting invading fleets before they were apparent to the naked eye.

Galileo went on to build larger and better telescopes, and when he turned his glass toward the sky, his observations not only greatly increased our knowledge of the heavens, but also upset the traditional beliefs of the earth as the center of the universe. Galileo discovered the mountains and craters of the moon's surface, the satellites of Jupiter, the Milky Way, and sun spots, and by showing that Venus has phases like Earth's moons, he destroyed the Ptolemaic theory that all heavenly bodies revolve around Earth.

From Galileo's time, the interest in telescopes and astronomy continued, and bigger and more powerful telescopes were built. In order to limit chromatic aberration (color distortions of and around an image), some refracting telescopes became incredibly long devices. One such telescope was 212 feet (64.6 m) long.

Today, the two largest refracting telescopes in the world are the 36-inch (91.4-cm) telescope at the Lick Observatory, built in 1888, and the 40-inch (101.6-cm) telescope at the Yerkes Observatory, built in 1898. Both are still in use.

In 1663, Isaac Newton devised a reflecting telescope, in which light is gathered and focused by a mirror. This was the beginning of a long line of reflecting telescopes.

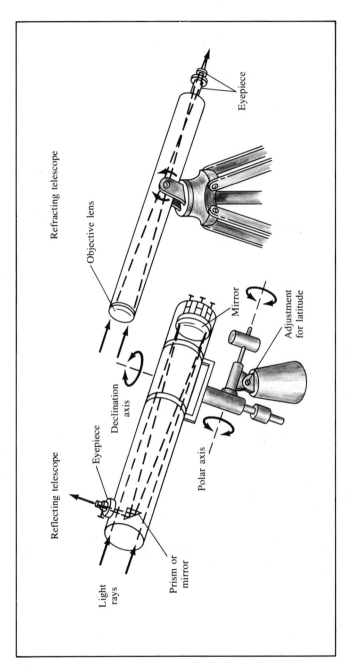

Figure 12. A comparison of the optical paths of reflecting and refracting telescopes.

Refracting telescope

Objective lens

Eyepiece

Reflecting telescope

Eyepiece

Declination axis

Mirror

Prism or mirror

Light rays

Polar axis

Adjustment for latitude

The mirror was made of speculum metal, a combination of tin, copper, and arsenic. The metal mirrors were not entirely successful, because they tarnished and had to be resurfaced and repolished frequently.

In the 1850s, the glass mirror reflector appeared, and when it was discovered that glass reflects much more light and, if tarnished, can be resilvered quite easily, the use of metal mirrors came to an end.

AMERICA'S
TELESCOPE BUILDER

The giant among twentieth-century telescope builders was an American, George Ellery Hale. At age twenty-four, he became director of the astronomical observatory at the University of Chicago. At that time the largest telescope in the world was the 36-inch refractor at the Lick Observatory.

Large 40-inch glass blanks had been manufactured to build a larger refracting telescope that would surpass the Lick Observatory's instrument. The University of Southern California had planned to buy the blanks by selling off some land given to them by a wealthy benefactor. The university planned to build an observatory on Mount Wilson, but when land prices in California crashed and the university was unable to purchase the glass blanks, Hale saw his opportunity. He convinced Charles Yerkes, a wealthy trolley-system owner, to underwrite the purchase of the glass blanks and build the observatory to house the proposed 40-inch telescope. Hale did not receive as much money from Yerkes as was promised, and considerable difficulty resulted.

The Yerkes Observatory finally opened in May 1897, on the shore of Lake Geneva, Wisconsin, and proved to be superior to the 36-inch Lick instrument.

Hale went through a traumatic experience shortly after the successful opening, when the huge elevator floor surrounding the telescope collapsed. Hale was very concerned that the telescope's lens had been damaged. At first glance, he thought the lens was cracked, but, fortunately, found out later that what at first appeared to be cracks were only a spider's web.

Hale realized that refracting telescopes would be limited to around 40 inches in diameter because larger sizes would necessitate thicker lenses, which would be less able to gather light.

He began planning for a larger, reflecting telescope. This time Hale's father gave him financial support by purchasing a 60-inch (152.4-cm) blank of glass for him. It was polished into a mirror at the Yerkes Observatory. At the same time Hale was purchasing the glass, his thoughts centered on where the new telescope should be housed. He decided that the ideal location would be the one the University of Southern California had chosen, Mount Wilson in California. He then turned his attention to finding other financial support for his new observatory. He finally received funds from the Carnegie Foundation to establish the Mount Wilson Solar Observatory.

In 1906, two years before the completion of the 60-inch mirrored telescope, Hale had approached another financial backer for support to build a 100-inch (254-cm) reflecting telescope. The 100-inch glass blank was received by Hale the very day the 60-inch mirror was set in place in the observatory on top of Mount Wilson.

In November 1916, the 100-inch reflector telescope began its work of exploring the sky. As in Hale's first experience with the Yerkes telescope, he experienced a tremendous scare. When he first used the telescope and focused on the planet Jupiter, he saw several overlapping images—workmen had left the telescope's cover open during the day, causing the mirror to heat up. Hale again wondered if the telescope was ruined. After letting it cool off, he focused the telescope on the star Vega and found that the image was very distinct and clear.

Hale's life of telescope building was not over yet. He soon envisioned a telescope twice the size of the 100-inch reflector on Mount Wilson. With funds from the Rockefeller Foundation, he began planning for a 200-inch (508-cm) telescope to be located on top of Mount Palomar in California. In 1938, ten years before the completion of the 200-inch reflector, Hale died.

For almost thirty years, the 200-inch Hale telescope was the largest telescope in the world. In the 1970s, a 240-inch (609.6-cm) Russian instrument, located in the Caucasus Mountains, became the largest of its type. For many years these two telescopes represented the state of the art in telescope building. The mirrors in both are made of Pyrex, a type of glass that is less affected by temperature than more common glass. Also, the mirrors were not made of a thick, heavy piece of glass, but were a relatively thin piece of glass, supported by a ribbed structure to support the glass. This made it possible to reduce the weight of the mirror considerably and also insured that temperature changes would equalize across the mirror much more rapidly.[18]

BIGGER AND BETTER EYES

We live in the golden age of astronomy. Not only are new observatories being built, but new types of telescopes are being constructed based on new techniques and technologies. While some technologies are used to enhance the capabilities of optical telescopes, many of these technologies enable us to view the sky in ways other than through the use of visible light.

One of the most interesting new approaches in telescope building is being carried out at the University of Arizona in Tucson, using a much different approach to making mirrors for optical telescopes. Mirrors are cast in a revolving furnace in which the molten, or liquid, glass assumes the form of a paraboloid. As the glass spins, the

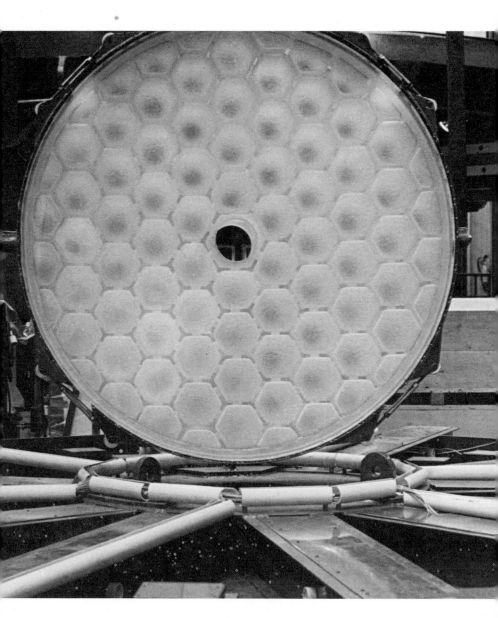

A 1.8-meter (6-ft) honeycomb telescope mirror blank made by Roger Angel of the University of Arizona using the spin-cast method.

centrifugal force pushes the molten glass to the outside of the mold. The curve of the mirror can then be programmed by the speed of the turntable. For deeper curves, a faster speed is used. Besides reducing the amount of time it takes to grind the mirror—from a few years to a few weeks—this process allows a much deeper curve, therefore a mirror of any focal length can be made.

Roger Angel, who perfected this method, has already successfully cast a 72-inch (182.9-cm) mirror and is presently preparing to cast several different size mirrors of up to a 256-inch (650.2-cm) mirror. In applying this new technology, Angel and his staff encountered a major problem in the beginning. As the first turntable was controlled by a console in the center of the turntable, the operators, who call themselves "oven pilots," suffered from motion sickness. The new turntable oven is now located under the University of Arizona's football stadium, and the control console is no longer in the center of the turntable.[19]

SIGHTING A SUPERNOVA

In February 1987, Ian Shelton, a Canadian astronomer, hit the proverbial astronomical jackpot while working at the University of Toronto's Las Campanas Observatory in Chile. While using the observatory's 10-inch (25.4-cm) telescope to take pictures of the large Magellanic Cloud, a galaxy, he noticed that on one of his photographic plates there was a bright spot that shouldn't have been there. When checking the photographic plates of his previous two nights' work, he saw that indeed a very bright star was present in his third plate that was only a faint image on the two previous nights. He had discovered the birth of a supernova, the first new observation since Kepler's discovery of a supernova in 1604.

This discovery had a great effect not only on Shelton's life, but on several subfields of astronomy as well. By the time that Shelton's discovery was logged into the central clearinghouse for astronomical discovery, the Harvard-Smithsonian Center for Astrophysics in Massachusetts, other astronomers around the world had noted the event and hastily begun their observations.[20]

RADIO TELESCOPES

One such group of astronomers were those who use interferometry to gather radio-wave data about objects in the universe. The process is to use two or more separate radio telescopes to gather radio signals from stars and combine the data. By combining the data the observer can deduce detail and structure too fine for a single radio telescope to register. Usually, the farther apart the telescopes, the greater the detail. In radio astronomy, this has been a common practice, and radio telescopes on Earth have even been linked to those in orbit.

The first use of a radio telescope was in 1931 when an American engineer pointed his antenna toward the sky and received what he correctly surmised were radio signals from the constellation Sagittarius. In 1940, Grote Reber published the first radio map of the Milky Way. After World War II, larger and larger radio telescopes were built, until today they range from the largest steerable disk of 328 feet (99.9 m) in Germany, to the largest meridian-transit disc of 300 feet (91.4 m) in West Virginia, to the 1,000-foot (304.8-m) spherical reflector in Puerto Rico. Even larger radio telescopes were built in the 1960s and 1970s using array antennas. Some of these antennas are almost one mile across. The one at Cambridge University, which is 3 miles (4.8 km) across, was used to discover pulsars (stars that emit bursts of microwaves on a regular basis) in 1967. The configuration of these large arrays of antennas differ, so that no one description fits them all. For example, some use grate-shaped antennas while a newer one in Australia uses parabolic reflectors about 40 feet (12.2 m) wide on arms, one mile in length. This radio

telescope, using interferometry, is responsible for the discovery of more than half of the known pulsars.

Today, astronomers are applying interferometrics techniques to telescopes, using visible light for imaging as well. This new technique was not possible until computers were used to continually monitor the telescope's image and make the necessary adjustments in the optics. Experiments have already shown that it can be applied to visible-light telescopes, and in the future not only will new information be gathered about galaxies and quasars but also individual stars will be imaged with greater precision and definition.

Once the radio astronomers were aware of the event of the supernova, they swung into action, especially those involved in very-long-baseline interferometry (VLBI), which requires coordination of radio telescopes often several thousand miles apart. They had to hurry to coordinate their efforts because the critical events of the supernova last from a few seconds to a few hours. Unfortunately, the radio astronomers using interferometry were unable to really see anything. Whether their instruments were pointed the wrong way, or the exploding star didn't emit enough radio energy to be detected, or the star was expanding so fast that the diameter of the star's shell had grown too large for the instrument is not yet known.

Other observers, using different techniques and instruments, were more fortunate in their observations. NASA's Kuiper Airborne Observatory is an instrumented plane that carries aloft a 36-inch infrared telescope. Because water vapor in the atmosphere absorbs infrared

A night view of the 210-foot-(64-m) diameter radio telescope in Parkes, Australia.

Some of the individual radio antennas that make up the Very Large Array radio telescope (VLA) near Socorro, New Mexico. This isolated area was chosen for its distance from air lanes. Radio waves from airplanes would interfere with those from the stars, which the observatory intercepts.

rays, the plane flies at altitudes that put the telescope above 99 percent of the earth's water vapor. This enables astronomers in the Southern Hemisphere to observe Shelton's supernova and a second bright object next to it that puzzles them. However, a cloud of matter ejected from the supernova obscures the view somewhat, and until it clears away, more precise observations will have to wait.

For one branch of space science, neutrino astronomy, Shelton's supernova gave scientists their first chance to observe an exploding star and the neutrinos it flings outward at very high speeds. Neutrinos are formed when, as the exploding star collapses from its immense weight, its atoms are crushed, forcing its electrons into the nuclei where they combine with protons to make neutrons. The neutrino particles are then emitted in tremendous numbers at the speed of light.

Scientists are immensely interested in neutrinos because they may answer the question of the universe's missing matter. It appears that 90 percent of the universe is made up of matter that is invisible or so-called dark matter. Astronomers believe this because calculations have shown that the visible matter in the universe is not nearly enough to account for the gravitational attraction at work in the universe. Russian scientists have pushed strongly their theory that this dark, or invisible, matter is made up of neutrinos, while other scientists believe that neutrinos have no rest mass and therefore could not be the invisible mass of the universe. If the Soviet scientists are correct, it will mean that our universe will someday stop expanding and start contracting. Massless neutrinos could mean that our universe would expand eternally.[21]

Neutrinos, with a low level of energy, are difficult to detect. There are, in fact, only a few neutrino detectors in the world. The detector, besides its sensing instruments, consists of a container of tons of water where the neutrinos can strike electrons or free protons, whereby they create what is called Cherenkov radiation (the light given off when a charged particle moves in a medium with a speed that is greater than that of light in that medium. Of the trillions of neutrinos created by the explosion of Shelton's supernova, observers at one science facility in Ohio estimated that 3,000 trillion neutrinos passed through their neutrino detector. Of that amount, only eight were actually detected, while eleven were detected at another observatory in Japan. Both the Japanese and American detectors recorded their observations at about the same time.

Though only nineteen neutrinos were recorded, they were enough to satisfy the scientists that some of their theories about neutrinos had validity, though it will take years of analysis to extract the meaning from all the information gathered.

PERFECTING OPTICAL TELESCOPES

Even with the advent of new types of astronomical instruments and procedures, the optical telescope has not been forgotten. Today larger and larger reflector telescopes are being built in order to extend our view of the universe from Earth. These telescopes are larger because of the new technologies in mirror construction, such as the spinning cast method or the use of multiple mirrors. Then, too, because these new mirrors are lighter and thinner than previous mirrors, their support structure need not be so massively heavy and thus they are less expensive.

There are two other approaches in mirror-making today. One is the use of multiple mirrors, where several smaller mirrors are used to gather the same amount of light as a single larger one would. For example, in one planned telescope, four 26.2-foot (8-m) mirrors combined would have the same light-gathering power as one 52.4-foot (16-m) mirror. The other approach is to have a single mirror made up of segmented hexagonal pieces of mirror to form a continuous mirror. In these two approaches to mirror-making, it then becomes crucial to control the multiple mirrors or segment surfaces very precisely.

In combining light from two or more sources, astronomers face enormous difficulties. One solution is to superimpose the two or more images so that the optical quality of the mirrors is not compromised. The other solution is to maintain phase—the process of keeping the light wave's crests and troughs in unison as they arrive from the mirrors. Certainly, if the optical telescope is to act as an interferometer, it must have phasing ability.

Phasing is nothing new in astronomy; it has been used in radio telescopes for years. Radio telescopes separated by continents have successfully matched wave fronts. However, optical telescopes have not been as successful because of the shortness of wavelengths involved. This fact makes it necessary that the crests of troughs of light be aligned 500,000 times more accurately than for radio waves.

In 1987, it was announced at a meeting of the American Astronomical Society that three astronomers had successfully tested a new optical metering system that solved the problems of superimposition and phasing. This system uses what is known as an optical bridge to bind together two adjacent mirrors. The bridge is formed when light from a xenon arc is bounced off the adjoining mirror edges. The beam, reflected from each mirror, passes through a prism that divides it into two parts. One part of the wave passes straight through the prism while the other part is deviated by a few arc seconds. The two light beams are reflected back from the top of the telescope to a detector at the bottom of the optical bridge. If all is in order, the wave fronts received by the detector will show three images. The center image, which has not been deviated by the prism, will show interference fringes. The other two images, if precisely superimposed, will be equidistant from the center image. If this is not the case, the image will be corrected by computer-controlled sensors either by varying the optical path or by tilting the telescope's secondary mirrors.[22]

Most people who looked at the sky through a large optical telescope would probably be disappointed in their view. It would little resemble the dazzling photographs of celestial objects that grace the pages of our science magazines. These are made possible through the use of photographic emulsions and use the telescope as a large camera. In order to capture the dim light of the objects in the sky, very long and often multiple exposures are necessary.

Though photographic plates have been used for over a century to record astronomical observations very well, they do have limitations. For example, photographic plates saturate with very long exposures and turn black. This also limits how well they can be used to measure the brightness of astronomical exposures. They are also nonlinear in character, that is, equal differences in exposure do not yield equal differences in the blackening of the photographic emulsion.

As a result of the limitations of photographic emulsions, astronomers have investigated the possibility of using other devices, such as electronic detectors. One electronic detector is the photomultiplier tube. When a photon, a light particle, is gathered by the telescope, it travels down to a light-sensitive surface inside of the photomultiplier tube. When the photon strikes the photocathode, it dislodges an electron, which, in turn, is attracted to a positively charged element called a dynode, and several more electrons are dislodged. After passing through several more dynodes, the original photoelectron has been amplified to a pulse of over a million electrons. This pulse is detected and recorded as a count. The photomultiplier is then used as a counter, and the number of counts recorded would be the measure of, for example, a star's brightness.

Another approach in improving the light-gathering

ability of telescopes is the application of a charge-coupled device (CCD), which is a photoconductive detector. CCDs can tremendously amplify the viewing power of a telescope. For example, a 36-inch telescope using CCDs can detect fainter objects than a 200-inch telescope using photographic plates. The CCD is made up of a silicon photosensitive surface and has the capacity to detect up to 70 percent of the photons striking it, making it much more sensitive than the fastest photographic film. As a photon strikes the surface of a CCD in the telescope, it frees an electric charge which is stored in the absorbing region. Once the exposure is complete, a readout of the CCD is done as to the amount of stored charge and also where in the CCD the charge is stored. Once a readout is done, the readout is transferred to a low-noise amplifier. The signals are then converted to digital data and stored in a computer memory to await analysis.

At present, CCDs respond to only a limited range of wavelengths, mostly in red and near-infrared regions. However, the use of fluorescent coating on CCDs holds great promise in extending their sensitivity to other wavelengths by converting incoming radiation to a frequency that CCDs can detect. Also under development is a CCD that can hold up to 4 million pixels (picture elements) that astronomers hope will help to expand their view of the universe.

Another new application of technology to telescopes is in the area of spectroscopy—the analysis of light. Using photographic plates in conjunction with the telescope to observe distant objects takes a great many hours. But today, through automation, the process is being speeded up. Using fiber optics, astronomers can analyze fifty or more objects at the same time. Some observatories use not only fiber optics, but use a robot to move the optical fibers into correct positions in the focal plane of the telescope.

Another new approach is the use of computer-controlled active optics. The newer computers have the capability of analyzing input data from the telescope and making decisions several times a second with great precision. For example, mirrors made up of segmented sections need to be aligned with each other to the millionth of an inch for proper imaging. The use of the computer and sensors makes this possible.[23]

One other approach in telescope-making is an old one that is being revived, the idea of a liquid telescope mirror. A Canadian astrophysicist, Ermanno Borra, has experimented with a mirror using a thin layer of mercury floating on a revolving form whose shape is configured as a paraboloid. The astronomer has already successfully tested a 3.2-foot (1-m) mirror and is planning a 7.2-foot (2.5-m) mirror. Though this approach has a serious disadvantage, that is, the mirror can only be pointed straight up, the advantage would be that the liquid mirrors would be very inexpensive to manufacture compared to conventional ones. Borra envisions a giant 98.4-foot (30-m) liquid mirror floating on water.

Today larger and larger reflector telescopes are being planned and built around the world to extend our view of the universe. As mentioned earlier, the 200-inch reflecting telescope at Mount Palomar in the United States and the 240-inch reflector in the Caucasus Mountains in the Soviet Union are the largest of their type today. However, their size will soon be surpassed.

One such telescope being built is the 32.8-foot (10-m)-diameter Keck telescope on top of Mauna Kea, a dormant volcano in Hawaii. The 13,796-foot (4,205-m) high mountain was chosen for the site of the new telescope for several

A model of the Keck telescope.
The human figures shown with the
model are the appropriate size
for the model's scale.

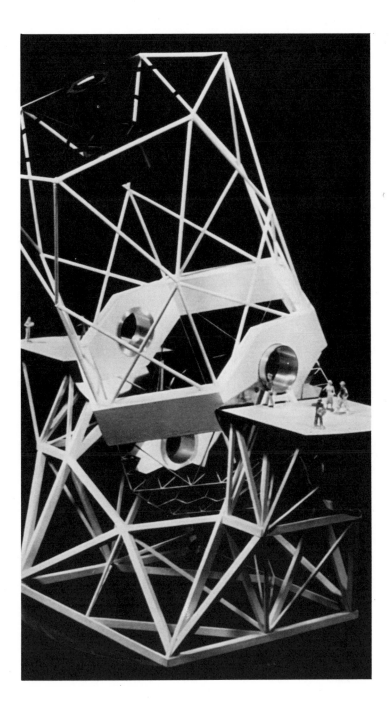

The Keck observatory dome under construction in October 1987. The observatory is scheduled to be completed in 1991.

reasons. First was the fact that the top of the volcano is above 40 percent of the earth's atmosphere and its air humidity level is one-tenth of that at sea level and allows for excellent viewing. Secondly, because the observatory is close to the equator, astronomers can view 90 percent of the known universe. An observatory at that elevation does have its limitations though. The oxygen level of the air is only half of that at sea level, forcing astronomers to retreat to a base camp 10,000 feet (3,048-m) below between shifts. Also, the wind sometimes reaches 100 miles (160.9 km) per hour at the peak, making it almost impossible for astronomers to walk from one observatory building to another.

The lens of the Keck telescope will be a segmented one, made up of thirty-six 5.7-foot (1.8-m) hexagonal mirrors to form the equivalent of a single 32.8-foot (10-m) mirror. The thirty-six segmented mirrors will be controlled by a computer using active optics to make the precise adjustments necessary to keep the mirrors aligned with each other. When the telescope begins operation, it will be the world's largest telescope mirror and will have three times the light-gathering power of the 19.6-foot (6-m) Soviet telescope. It will be able to see the light of a single candle from the distance of the moon.

Many other very large multiple-mirror telescopes are being planned. One such is the U.S. National New Technology Telescope (NNTT), patterned after the successful Multiple Mirror Telescope (MMT) in Arizona. It will consist of four 26.2-foot (8-m) mirrors, equivalent to a 52.4-foot (16-m) mirror.

To yield a 52.4-foot (16-m) image, all four mirrors will be focused to a common point. The mirrors can also be operated independently to get four images of the same object. This would allow astronomers to observe the object being examined at different wavelengths. The NNTT will also have state-of-the-art instrumentation—a wide-angle CCD camera; a cooled, very low temperature, high-

The multiple-mirror telescope (MMT) located on Mount Hopkins, Arizona. The telescope consists of six 72-inch (182.9-cm) mirrors.

resolution spectrograph; infrared imaging devices; and a multiple object spectrograph.

Building the NNTT will be very expensive. However, astronomers believe that it will be well worth the expense, because it will extend our vision of the universe many times over. For example, it will be able to image stars as faint as the twenty-eighth magnitude and will outperform today's 13.1-foot (4-m) reflectors by 1.5 times in examining galaxies. Further, the NNTT will have very high resolution when used as an interferometer and also offers impressive gains over present telescopes in high-speed spectroscopy. It is expected that in infrared imaging, the NNTT would be twice as effective as the 32.8-foot (10-m) Keck telescope.

While the Americans are planning the NNTT, the Europeans are planning their answer to it in what is called the Very Large Telescope (VLT). The VLT will have four 26.2-foot (8-m) mirrors which, combined, will have the light-gathering power of a 52.4-foot (16-m) mirror. Unlike the NNTT, the VLT is designed for open-air operation and each mirror will be mounted separately. When used as an interferometer, the VLT will be in a class by itself because the individual mountings of its mirrors make possible a baseline 521.6 feet (159 m) long—seven times more powerful in this regard than the NNTT. It is expected that the VLT will be completed by the end of this century.

Among other telescopes being planned is the Columbus Project or the "two-shooter." It is to have two 26.2-foot (8-m) telescopes in tandem, like binoculars, equal in light-gathering power to a 37.6-foot (11.5-m) reflector.

Scheduled for completion in 1990 is a 26.2-foot (8-m) telescope being built at the Las Campanas Observatory in Chile. This instrument will consist of only a single mirror. From its location in the Southern Hemisphere, it will have a clear view of the Magellanic Clouds and the center of our own galaxy.

One telescope that reflects the new technology is the 11.4-foot (3.5-m) New Technology Telescope (NTT), located in the European Southern Observatory in La Silla, Chile. This telescope features thin-mirror construction to reduce costs. Because the thin, 9.4-inch (24-cm) slab of glass-ceramic distorts easily, corrections must be made in the mirror's surfaces through the use of sensors that apply pressure to the mirror and are controlled by a computerized optic system. Additionally, the telescope can be operated from the European Southern Observatory's headquarters in Garching, West Germany.

Other types of telescopes have been developed and constructed in recent years that are specialized in their approach to astronomy. The McMath Solar Telescope at the Kitt Peak Observatory in Arizona is one of these specialized instruments. By using a long focal length of 300 feet (91 m) and a large mirror 80 inches (203 cm) in diameter, images of the sun 3 feet (.9 m) in diameter are obtained. As long as the weather isn't cloudy, this instrument allows scientists to observe the sun for spots, flares, and prominences.

As good as these earthbound instruments are in imaging objects in the universe, they are often greatly hampered by the earth's atmosphere. Water vapor blocks infrared rays, while the atmosphere itself causes stellar images to scintillate and blocks other rays of interest. Additionally, the atmosphere is not as clean as it once was, and telescopes located near highly populated areas are affected by light from cities and towns. And, of course, cloudy or overcast skies inhibit observation. As good as our present astronomical instruments are, none has the ability to inspect closely the surfaces of the other planets in our solar system. Therefore, it becomes evident that astronomical instruments must be lifted above our atmosphere or even be put into space for clearer and truer images.[24]

SIX

EYES IN SPACE

In the first attempts to observe the universe free from the inhibiting effects of the earth's atmosphere, balloons were used to carry astronomical instruments aloft. As early as 1911, Victor Hess, an Austrian physicist, used a balloon to lift an electroscope, a device that measures radiation, some 1,600 feet (487.7 m) and inadvertently discovered cosmic rays. Twenty years later, the Swiss physicist Auguste Picard developed a balloon that rose 10 miles (16 km) high. Picard's balloon used helium as the lifting agent and had a sealed aluminum gondola that, when pressurized, served as a suitable environment for humans. In the 1970s, balloons reached a height of 25 miles (40.2 km), which meant that 99.9 percent of the earth's atmosphere was below the balloon.

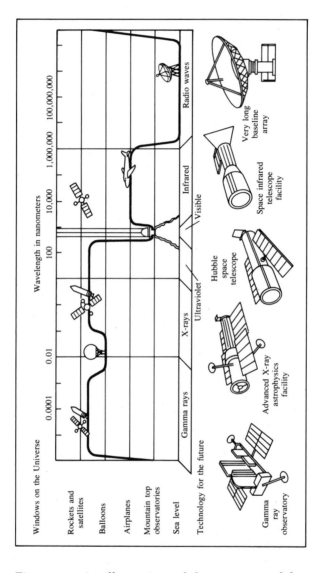

Figure 13. An illustration of the present and future telescopes that will be used to measure the various wavelengths of energy, and an illustration of the transparency of the atmosphere to wavelengths of electromagnetic energy.

In 1964, John Strong, an American physicist, using a special telescope elevated 16 miles (25.7 km) observed water vapor in the clouds of Venus. Another astronomer discovered that Mars, too, has a small amount of water vapor. In 1957, a remote-controlled telescope was lifted by a balloon 15 miles (24.1 km) into the atmosphere and focused on the sun to image it more sharply than ever before. In 1970, an unmanned balloon, *Stratoscope II*, reached the altitude of 80,000 feet (24,385 m), where its 36-inch (91.4-cm) reflector telescope focused on the planet Uranus. The pictures were so clear that for the first time the planet's "limb darkening"—a gradual decrease in luminosity toward its edges—was seen. Also, the planet's equatorial bulge was measured to a new degree of accuracy.

As good as balloons were in hoisting astronomical instruments to clearer views, they were limited. Though they opened up new vistas for infrared imaging, they were unable to get high enough to study solar wind and the ultraviolet radiation of the sun and the stars, which was stopped by the upper ranges of the atmosphere. Clearly, a new way was needed to get beyond the earth's atmosphere and that way was at hand—rockets.

Rockets were invented by the Chinese in the thirteenth century. The British used rockets as weapons against the Americans in the War of 1812. Robert Goddard, an American physicist, started to experiment with rockets in 1923. His purpose was to build rockets not as weapons, but for the exploration of space. In 1939, Goddard, using liquid fuel to power his rockets, was finally able to fire rockets that went faster than the speed of sound and reached an altitude of 1.5 miles (2.4 km).

Meanwhile, in Germany, a group interested in rocketry was founded. Two of its leaders were Willie Ley and Wernher von Braun. Once Hitler came to power in Germany, he saw the advantages of using rockets as weapons, and by 1936 a secret base had been built in Germany to advance the use of rocketry in warfare. By the end of

World War II, the Germans were bombarding England on regular basis with V-2 missiles, large rocket-powered bombs. As the war ended, the Soviet Union and the United States rushed to capture Germany's rocket experts. Von Braun and his colleagues surrendered to the Americans.

THE RACE TO SPACE

With the capture of German rocket scientists and V-2 rockets, the United States began space research. By 1949, a small, second-stage rocket mounted on a V-2 rocket was able to reach an altitude of 240 miles (386.2 km). That was high, but not high enough. Then, too, the rockets and their instruments were able to gather information about the stars and planets for only short periods of time. A more permanent observation post was needed. In 1957, the Soviet Union launched the first artificial satellite—*Sputnik 1*. Though *Sputnik 1* did not do much more than send out a signal, its ramifications were felt around the world.

A month later, *Sputnik 2* was rocketed into space by the Russians. In the capsule was a dog; its heartbeat was monitored from the ground by telemetry. When the batteries ran down, the dog was put to death. On January 31, 1958, the Americans answered the two Russian launches with their own, *Explorer 1*. Because of miniaturization, *Explorer 1* was a much smaller satellite than the Russian Sputniks. It was packed with instruments to record cosmic rays and other charged particles in space. Later in 1958, *Explorer 3* and *Sputnik 3* sent back data indicating that at certain altitudes above the earth the radiation count dropped to zero. James Van Allen, the American space scientist, did not believe these readings to be accurate and felt that the recording instruments might have been adversely affected by existing radiation. So, when *Explorer 4* was sent up in July 1958, its instruments were shielded against radiation. This time the instruments told a different story, and the first important discovery rendered possible by rocketry was made, that the earth was surrounded by radiation belts, at first called the "Van Allen belts" and later the magnetosphere.[25]

Over the next few years, the Russians launched several of their Luna series of rockets toward the moon. In 1959, *Luna 1* passed close to the moon, and in the same year *Luna 2* actually struck the moon's surface. In October 1959, *Luna 3* passed behind the moon, taking pictures. For the first time, humans were able to see the far side of the moon. Interestingly, it was found by other Luna rockets and the American *Lunar Orbiter I* that the far side of the moon differed greatly from the side toward the earth. The Lunar orbiters were able to ultimately map the entire surface of the moon with great precision. In 1966, the Russians, with their *Luna 9*, and the Americans, with *Surveyor 1*, made soft landings on the moon to photograph the surface and chemically analyze the surface, too.

LOOKING BEYOND THE MOON

The first great planetary probe was carried out in 1962 by the American *Mariner 2* space probe. Its mission was to pass by the planet Venus and measure properties of the planet. Upon approaching to within 21,680 miles (32,187 km) of the planet, *Mariner 2* discovered that Venus had no magnetosphere and that the surface of the planet was very hot, 800° F (427° C), thus confirming earthbound observation. Unfortunately, *Mariner 2* carried no imaging equipment and no pictures were possible.

All of the Mariners launched to Mars, though, were equipped with imaging systems. In 1965, *Mariner 4* passed within 6,500 miles (10,460 km) of the surface of Mars and took twenty-one pictures that destroyed many of the myths about the Martian landscape. It was discovered that there were no canals as previously thought, but a landscape as stark as the moon's. Images of Mars recorded by *Mariner 6* and *7* further reinforced the finding that Mars looked like the lunar highlands. In 1971, *Mariner 9*, the first human-made object to orbit a planet other than Earth, went into orbit around Mars and systematically mapped it from pole to pole. From this mapping, it was found that earlier probes had not truly sampled Mars's surface and that Mars was indeed an evolved body. Enormous volcanoes and canyons were discovered, and deposits of dust and ice at both poles seemed to indicate that Mars may have had a relatively recent climate change.

In our search for life on the other planets, flybys and orbiting probes have provided us with a comprehensive body of physical data from which to draw conclusions. We already knew that Mars was the most promising of the other planets to have life, for it had nitrogen, carbon, and water vapor, the necessary ingredients for life on Earth. The American space scientists decided to leapfrog the systematic approach to the problem of life on Mars and go directly to the planet itself. In 1976, the Viking landers made the historic *Mariner 9* mission look primitive. The Viking probes, complete with laboratories, were able to land on the surface of Mars and perform experiments upon the Martian soil. The soil samples, garnered at two widely separated sites and processed by the biological laboratories of the Vikings, showed that there were no living organisms in the soil and no organic material to the parts-per-billion level.

Other space probes that added to our knowledge of the planets were *Pioneer 10*, which in 1973 passed by Jupiter at a distance of 85,000 miles (136,795 km); *Mariner 10*, which in 1974 passed within 21,700 miles (34,920 km) of the surface of Mercury (its images showed that the planet's surface was as heavily cratered as the moon's, and instruments indicated that the planet had a weak magnetic field); and *Pioneer 11*, which in 1974 surveyed Jupiter at

An artist's rendition of the Mariner *spacecraft's journey through space to Jupiter and Saturn.*

a distance of 28,000 miles (45,060 km) on its way to Saturn. Both of the Pioneer space probes were able to take pictures of the satellites of Jupiter.

Two of the most amazing planetary probes launched by the United States in the late summer and early fall of 1977 were *Voyagers 1* and *2*. In January 1986, *Voyager 2* passed close by Uranus and, still fully operable, sent back to Earth pictures and instrument readings about the planet and its fifteen moons. For *Voyager 2*, this was the third planet in our solar system that it had been able to inspect in its long voyage, while its companion ship, *Voyager 1*, has flown by Jupiter and Saturn. As amazing as these feats were, it is expected that both probes will, barring accidents and equipment failure, continue to send back information to Earth until the year 2015.[26]

Both Voyagers have encountered planetary dangers beyond our imaginations. When these two spacecraft approached Jupiter some four months apart, both probes faced extremely high levels of radiation. Both were pelted with icy particles while they discovered the unknown rings of Saturn. In their travels they have given scientists warning that future space probes should be strongly shielded against radiation.

In 1986, scientists were jubilant when *Voyager 2* passed by Uranus, as *Voyager 1* and *2* were initially de-

A photograph of Jupiter taken February 1, 1979 by Voyager I *at a range of 20 million miles (32.7 million kilometers). Jupiter's Great Red Spot, observed for hundreds of years by astronomers, but never in such detail, is shown here.*

signed to last only long enough to explore Jupiter and Saturn. When *Voyager 2* passed by Uranus it was moving at a speed of 35,000 miles per hour (56,325 kph)—a speed too fast for the transmission of clear images. Scientists on Earth, making adjustments to their monitoring devices so that the images taken by Voyager would not be blurred, were able to receive even better pictures than those the spacecraft had sent from Jupiter and Saturn. Through images and readings, *Voyager 2* sent back to Earth information on Uranus's belt of high-energy charged particles, its pitch-black rings, its fifteen moons, and its complex geological history.

Voyager 1's trajectory is such that it will not encounter any other planets of the solar system. However, *Voyager 2* will pass by Neptune in the late summer of 1989, and if all is working well, it will transmit pictures and instrument readings of that planet. Both space probes will then leave our solar system, heading toward deep space. Though neither is directed toward nearby stars, both Voyagers have affixed on the outside of the spacecraft a phonograph record containing 116 pictures in digital form representing our science, technology, institutions, and music, and an essay on the evolution of Earth. Whether these records will ever be heard or understood by alien beings is debatable, but if these spacecraft are ever intercepted by aliens and our record is understood, it will probably be several thousand years in the future.[27]

Many of these unarmed space probes were setting the stage for the Apollo missions. The dominant purpose of the Apollo flights—to send people to the moon—was not a scientific one. The astronauts did, however, bring back several hundred pounds of lunar samples, from which we have learned some things about the moon's origins. We know the major events that shaped the moon's surface. First came the chemical separation of the crust, followed 500 million years later by the gigantic impacts of meteors, comets, and asteroids that produced the basins and their flooding by lava. Then some 3 billion years ago, as charted by volcanism, there was a tailing-off of the geologic activity. We also know that the moon's lithosphere (crust), is 600 miles deep and there is little seismic activity.

The future of exploring space with probes, landers, and space telescopes seems promising. Though the explosion of the space shuttle *Challenger* in January 1986 has slowed progress, space probe plans are going forward, and spacecraft and instruments of extraordinary power are being built. Four of the most prominent extensions of the scientists' views are the Hubble Space Telescope, the Galileo space probe, the Ulysses probe, and the Mars Observer probe.

INFRARED ASTRONOMY

Though many earthbound telescopes have infrared detectors, there are serious problems in their use. One is that all objects—including the telescope, the buildings surrounding it, and even the sky—radiate infrared radiation. To protect the detector from the warmth of infrared radiation, it must be cooled to very low temperatures of $-392°$ F $(-200°$ C$)$ or below. Ordinarily this is done by cooling the detector with liquid nitrogen or helium, and if a lower temperature is desired, a vacuum pump is used to lower the pressure over liquid helium. The detector is enclosed in a metal container with a tiny viewing window and surrounded by the liquid helium. Since even tiny bits of dust are sources of infrared radiation, the optics must be kept very clean.

Another problem is the earth's atmosphere itself, especially the water vapor. Infrared observations should be made at the highest elevation with the lowest humidity possible and in cloud-free skies, as even the thinnest cloud emits a large amount of radiation. Today, most infrared telescopes are located in observatories at elevations above 9,800 feet (3,000 m). The observatory at Mauna Kea in

Hawaii, at an elevation of over 13,000 feet (4,200 m), houses two of the largest infrared telescopes.

A better way to make infrared observations is from airplanes at high altitudes or from space. The first airborne infrared observations were made in the 1960s using a Lear jet and a 12-inch (30.5-cm) telescope that made observations through a hole cut in the side of the plane. Today, the Gerard P. Kuiper Airborne Observatory (see pages 93–94), which is named for a pioneer in infrared astronomy, is NASA's infrared observatory. A 3.2-foot (1-m) telescope is mounted in a Lockheed C-141 that flies some sixty to one hundred days a year at altitudes of 40,000 to 44,000 feet (12,000–13,500 m) making observations. The cooled telescope is mounted on an air bearing to minimize vibration and is computer controlled. NASA is now planning a second infrared telescope of at least 6.5 feet (2 m) to be housed in a Boeing 747.[28]

Infrared astronomical observations are probably best made from space. Not only does this free the detector from the water vapor in the earth's atmosphere, it also allows the entire optical system to be cooled to reduce nearly all radiation from the optics and allow observations in the longer wavelengths of the infrared spectrum.

The first real infrared space-launched laboratory was the Infrared Astronomy Satellite (IRAS) in early 1983. IRAS was a joint venture of the United States, Britain, and the Netherlands. For ten months, the liquid-helium-cooled telescope made a survey of the entire sky under optimum conditions. Unfortunately, at the end of ten months the supply of liquid helium coolant was exhausted.

The data gathered by IRAS resulted in a bonanza for astronomers specializing in infrared analysis. Some of the data are still being analyzed today and will be for several more years. A major discovery of IRAS was that there is a ring of dust and debris surrounding the star Vega, enough to form several times the number of planets in our solar system. It appears that IRAS discovered several other stars with debris systems like Vega.

Confirmation of the nature of IRAS's discoveries will have to wait until the launch of the Space Infrared Telescope Facility (SIRTF). SIRTF will have ten times better angular resolution than IRAS and will have the capability of making infrared pictures of the faintest infrared sources found by IRAS. The one-meter class telescope will be operated as part of a space station or some sort of space orbital platform and, as a result, its supply of liquid helium can be continually replenished, unlike IRAS's.

IRAS was a survey instrument. SIRTF will be a true observatory. It will be able to cover the entire infrared spectrum. Because of advances in technology, its detectors will be made more sensitive than those of IRAS, and since it will carry a variety of focal instruments, it will be capable of extensive observations of a single object. After SIRTF is launched, astronomers will be able to confirm the nature and amount of debris surrounding those planetary bodies exhibiting infrared excess.

HIGH-ENERGY ASTRONOMY

Not until after World War II was one area of astronomical investigation possible, that of high-energy radiation. Because the earth's atmosphere blocks electromagnetic radiation of wavelengths less than 3000 Å, X-ray, and ultraviolet, and gamma-ray observations must be made from space. In 1946, using captured German rockets, the United States began flights to observe the sun's far ultraviolet radiation.

Since the 1960s, the United States and other countries have launched earth satellites to make astronomical observations of high-energy radiation. These included such devices as orbiting solar observatories, orbiting astronomical observatories, high-energy astronomy observatories,

SkyLab, and most recently, the European Spacelab. Between 1962 and 1975, eight satellites were launched containing orbital solar observatories to collect data about the sun's ultraviolet-ray, X-ray, and gamma-ray emissions. In 1980, a major solar space observatory, the Solar Maximum Satellite, was launched. Electronic failures disabled the craft a few months later; however, in 1984 repairs were made by astronauts of the space shuttle, enabling Solar Max to resume operation.

X rays are emitted from gas at very high temperatures and consist of electromagnetic radiation wavelengths of less than 120 Å. There are two types of X rays: soft X rays that are of lower energy (longer wavelengths) and hard X rays of higher energy (shorter wavelengths). The first observations of X rays from space were first made by instruments in high-altitude balloons and rockets. In 1970, the first orbiting X-ray satellite was launched, named *Uhuru*, a Swahili term for freedom. During its operational life of three years, *Uhuru* charted over two hundred X-ray sources.

Between 1977 and 1979, the United States launched three High Energy Astronomy Observatories, HEAO-1, HEAO-2, and HEAO-3. HEAO-1 did not produce images, but through the use of a gas-ionization detector, did detect the presence and intensity of X rays from a certain direction. In 1978, HEAO-2, or the Einstein Observatory, was launched, advancing X-ray astronomy dramatically. Because X rays are easily absorbed by optics, the X-ray telescope in Einstein was built much differently to measure incoming X rays. A complex set of mirrors were angled in such a way that the X rays would graze the mirrors and be reflected and focused into an actual X-ray image. The Einstein was then able to detect weak X-ray sources over one thousand times weaker than had been previously detected. HEAO-3, launched in 1979, is being used to detect cosmic, or high-energy, space particles.

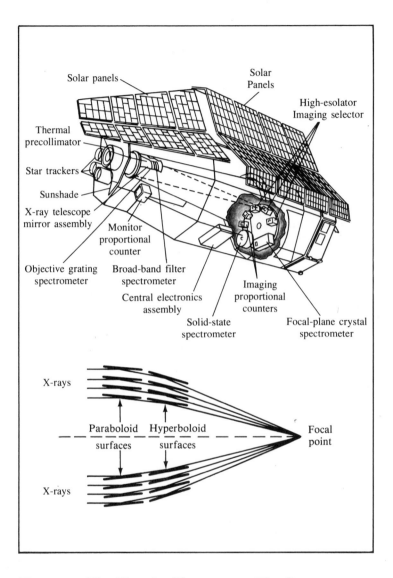

Figure 14. The Einstein Observatory. The diagram at the bottom of the illustration shows how an X-ray telescope works. When X rays are reflected from specially-angled surfaces, the rays come to a focus.

The highest energy photons are known as gamma rays. These rays were first discovered in nuclear reactions. The first gamma-ray investigations were carried on through the use of giant balloons carrying detectors high into the atmosphere. Later, because of the military's interest in surveillance of nuclear reactions, the first orbiting gamma-ray detectors were military ones. The Vela satellite system was the first one to discover gamma rays of cosmic origin. In 1967, the Vela satellite detected mysterious flashes of low-energy gamma-ray radiation, the origin of which is unknown. Investigations into high-energy gamma-ray radiation began with the second Orbiting Solar Observatory, but the first sensitive surveys were accomplished by the second Small Astronomy Satellite on the European Space Agency's gamma-ray telescope. These two surveys found that there were many places in our galaxy producing tremendous amounts of electromagnetic radiation. The nature of the sources of these gamma rays is not yet known; however, three sources have been found: pulsars, quasars, and cosmic rays, interacting with atoms in a giant molecular cloud.

Astronomers are planning further investigation into high-energy radiation with a number of space observatories and telescopes. The Hubble Space Telescope, to be launched within the next few years, will investigate infrared and ultraviolet radiation. Also scheduled to be launched soon is the Gamma Ray Observatory, which will provide us with an in-depth look at gamma rays. The Advanced X-Ray Astrophysics Facility (AXAF) could be launched by the end of this century and give astronomers an even better understanding of these rays than the highly successful Einstein X-ray satellite.[29]

The Hubble Space Telescope (HST) was first known as the Large Space Telescope (LST). Since it was originally proposed, though, its name has been changed to honor the astronomer Edwin Hubble, the proponent of the idea that the universe is expanding. The HST, already complete, awaits a ride into orbit around the earth. The telescope, 43 feet (13.1 m) long and 14 feet (4.2 m) wide at its broadest point, weights 12.75 tons. It houses a 94-inch (2,387-cm) reflecting mirror, six instruments, and an electronics system to view the far reaches of the universe.

The 94-inch mirror is believed to be an excellent light collector, though there has been some concern over dust collecting on the mirror, and it has had to be cleaned once already. Instruments on the HST include five guidance sensors capable of precise astronometric observations; a faint-object camera; a high-speed photometer; a wide-field and planetary camera; a faint-object spectrograph; and a high-resolution spectrograph.

Scientists are worried that there won't be enough to enable the HST to carry out all its designated functions. At present two huge wings attached to the HST will contain 2,438 solar cells generating over 4,000 watts of electricity. Some engineers working on the project believe that this is not enough power to meet the needs of the HST when working in orbit. Already, there are some indications that more efficient solar cells will have to be substituted for the ones already in place.

When the HST is placed into orbit by the shuttle orbiter *Atlantis*, a new vista in astronomy will be opened. The HST will be able to detect objects 1/100 as bright as those visible from the 200-inch Palomar telescope on Earth. It will be able to see ten times farther into the universe than ever before, and it will be able to gather information about the ultraviolet and infrared regions with unparalleled precision. With its ability to see a billion light-years into space, the HST may resolve whether, as its namesake Hubble proposed, the universe in indeed expanding forever or that expansion is slowing and the universe may collapse someday and start all over again.[30]

The purpose of the Ulysses spacecraft is to explore the sun. The plasma and energetic particles in the polar regions of the sun are relatively unknown. No spacecraft has ever directly measured these areas and the scientific problem posed is whether the magnetic field configuration on the sun resembles those of the polar regions on Earth.

The Galileo orbiter will be sent to Jupiter in the near future to gain new information and refine information from previous flybys like the Voyagers. Not only will Galileo go into orbit around Jupiter, it will also launch four probes into the planet's atmosphere. Sometime after the Galileo, similar exploration is slated for Saturn. Scientists are looking forward to both of these probes because both Jupiter and Saturn are formed predominantly of hydrogen and helium but have apparently evolved in very different ways. Also, two moons of Jupiter, Io and Europa, are of great interest to us because they differ markedly from the other moons of Jupiter. Io and Europa both have young surfaces; Io has intense volcanism whereas Europa's surface is being shaped by ice.

The one planned exploration that is in the best position to be launched on time is the Mars Observer spacecraft, scheduled for launch in 1990. It will be the first American probe to Mars since 1976 when *Viking Lander 1* landed on Mars's Plain of Gold. Even though American and Russian space probes have landed on the surface of Mars, our scientific knowledge of the planet is minimal. We do not yet know about the thickness of the planet's surface, the nature of its mantle, or even if the core is molten.

The Mars Observer will try to answer many questions about the red planet. By using cameras and instruments in an orbit of 225 miles (362 km) above the surface, the satellite will gather information about the composition of the planet's surface. A complete map of Mars will be made over a 200-day period. A global picture of weather conditions will be made every day by cameras on the craft. Detailed photos of Mars will be taken by a camera that can differentiate structures of only a few feet in diameter. Other instruments will be used to determine the composition of Mars's atmospheric dust; the location, temperature, height, and amount of water vapor in Martian clouds; and the composition, behavior, and physical properties of the planet's polar caps.

There are other space projects that are in either the planning or construction stage that are intended to extend our view of the universe. When the space shuttle flies again, experiments will resume, using humans and instruments to probe space. The Magellan Venus radar-mapper spacecraft will be launched in the near future to map the cloud-covered surface of Venus, using radar. Some astronomers are already planning a space telescope of 32.8 feet (10 m) to be put into orbit, while other scientists are envisioning mobile laboratories on Mars's surface to analyze and collect samples for return to Earth. A shuttle/ Centaur rocket launch is also planned in the near future for an orbit-matching rendezvous with a comet. Besides our own endeavors, other countries, like the Soviet Union, with a strong space exploration program, and Japan and several European countries, will continue to extend their view of our universe.[31]

REMOTE SENSING

Most people believe that the launching of *Sputnik 1* in 1957 was the beginning of remote sensing from space of the earth's geography. Remote sensing is the acquisition of physical data in a manner that does not involve direct contact in any way. Early attempts to remotely sense images date from over 2,300 years ago when Aristotle experimented with a "camera obscura." In the 1850s, photographs were taken of Earth from a balloon, using the photographic process of Daguerre, beginning the modern-day imaging of earth from above. Since 1957, several thousand satellites have been put into orbit around Earth for the purpose of observing and recording Earth's land masses and oceans, its climate, and its atomic explosions. They have even been used as navigational aids.

Earth-orbiting satellites lead dangerous lives. They must survive the pressures of blast-off and the possibility of the rocket's blowing up at launch. Some, after surviving the launch, go into improper orbit and even disappear into deep space. Once in orbit, they must be constantly monitored from the ground for fluctuations in orbit caused by solar flares, gravity, and the fact that the dark and sunlit sides of the vehicle will vary some 300 degrees in temperature. The internal electronics and equipment must be monitored as well. If a course correction is needed, small fuel jets can be triggered from Earth to change course, but only sparingly, because the fuel supply is limited. As a result of these stresses, the life of satellites is limited. At the end of the satellite's life, the controllers on Earth will often try to kick the satellite into higher orbit to keep orbital paths clear. Most satellites end their careers in flames as they fall back into the earth's atmosphere—with only one known fatality on Earth, a cow in Cuba.

LOOKING AT
EARTH FROM ABOVE

The United States has orbited a number of satellites to examine the earth's surface. A series of satellites, named Landsat, have added immensely to our knowledge of the earth. Landsat is now called EOSAT since it is gradually being turned over from the U.S. government to a private company. Many were skeptical that a craft 570 miles (917.2 km) in the atmosphere could add to our knowledge—but how wrong they were. Landsat and other orbiters were able to map the world completely by satellite photos and make many important discoveries at the same time. Maps that had shown objects like rivers, lakes, and mountains in the wrong positions for hundreds of years were corrected. Unknown lakes and geological features were charted. Landsat discovered a new islet, an uncharted reef in the Indian Ocean, and was responsible for locating deposits of oil and minerals. Landsat even redefined state borders.

These satellites are also useful in taking inventory and monitoring land resources. In doing this, from a remote spacecraft, two approaches are used. The first is to identify the specific attributes of a resource complex. The second is to determine what differences exist in one component or another of a total resource complex. This information is vitally important for foresters and agriculturists, geologists, hydrologists, and geographers.

Foresters and agriculturists are basically interested in the amount and distribution of the biomass and ecosystems, especially the types, vigor, and changes of vegetation. Geologists are interested in the worldwide distribution of geomorphic features, and specifically interested in the location of mineral and oil deposits. Hydrologists' basic interests are in the quantitative factors involved in the hydrologic and climate cycles, and specifically in the location of, and suitable sites for, storage of water. Geographers are interested in global, regional, subregional, and local land-use patterns as well as the nature and extent of changes in vegetation, animal populations, and human settlement throughout the world. Geographers want to know the location of transportation and communication facilities, economic activities of specific areas, and land use and production of Earth's resources. Satellites have given, and are giving us, this information.

Not only are scientists interested in observing and imaging the earth's crust, but they are also very interested in gathering information about the world's oceans. The traditional method of gathering information about the oceans has been through the use of ships and moored buoys, an expensive method. In 1978, NASA launched a satellite called Seasat, whose mission was devoted solely to oceanography. The satellite carried four new microwave sensors and operated for three months during 1979.

The application of remote sensing to the earth's oceans is varied. One of the great interests of scientists was in learning more about the oceans' role in weather and climate. Since the oceans can hold far more heat for a longer time than can land masses, they moderate climates north and south of the equator considerably. Where ocean temperatures fluctuate, they play an important role in producing variations in climate. Also of great importance are the surface winds of the ocean. Seasat carried a radar device called a scatterometer to transmit microwaves and measure the amount scattered back from waves and other rough features of the ocean that influence wind speed and direction. Sea ice plays an important role, too, in the earth's weather since it covers some 13 percent of the oceans. Remote-sensing devices have enabled us, for the first time, to gain an immediate knowledge of the variations of sea-ice cover.

Though remote sensing cannot tell whether fish are present in large numbers in any particular area of an ocean, it can give us other information that may be helpful in locating marine life. This is done by a more basic biological approach, the analysis of the ocean's color, which indicates the presence or lack of algae or phytoplankton. These drifting microorganisms are the basis of the entire marine food chain, and often when the ocean's color reflects large amounts of the organisms to remote sensors, fish will be present, too.

Remote sensors are able to distinguish whether surface pollutants, such as oil, are present in water. Substances deeper in the water have been more difficult to detect. Satellites can sense, at times, ocean-dumped wastes and suspended sediments. To obtain a quantitative measure of pollutants, boats still must be used to gather water samples.

Landsat and other scanners already have proved valuable in locating mineral deposits on land masses. Remote sensing in marine geophysics has proved more difficult to accomplish and is still in the developmental stage. As would be expected, there is a high degree of commercial interest in locating mineral and oil deposits in the world's oceans. Seasat's radar altimeter was used to develop global maps of the earth's gravity field. The radar altimeter was able to measure, with precision, the height of the ocean's surface. Since the height, or relief, of the surface is largely a measure of the earth's gravity field, seamounts and dense rocks on the ocean's floor will cause the surface of the ocean to bulge upward by an amount that is measurable. This technique has been used to produce maps giving valuable information about the composition of the ocean floor. Over the next ten years, American, European, and Japanese satellites will be launched and soon afterward will yield information about the ocean floor, so that mining and oil exploration applications of remote sensors may become profitable.[32]

A very important date in remote sensing of the earth was May 20, 1960. *Tiros 1*, the first weather satellite, sent back to Earth an image of a unique cloud system stretching from Hawaii to the Great Lakes. This was the beginning of the technique to map weather systems, over both land and oceans. Until *Tiros 1* orbited Earth, we were relatively ignorant of weather patterns over large expanses of oceans. Today, several countries' weather satellites image the entire globe every half hour, night and day, greatly improving our short-term forecasting ability.

There are a number of factors that affect weather: the oceans' temperature, the amount of atmospheric dust and volcanic particles, variations of snow and ice, evaporation, and human activity. Because the remote sensors we have today cannot accurately gauge all of these factors, and because we do not have the ability to translate these data into meaningful models, weather forecasting is often problematical. In an experiment carried out in 1979 as part of the Global Atmospheric Research Program, using seven satellites and weather buoys and balloons, it was discovered that the temperature soundings and wind-speed determination of satellites were in substantial error. It seems then that even though satellites have had tremendous impact on weather forecasting, substantial work needs to be done before the theoretical upper limit of fourteen days can be reached in building forecast models. A long-term goal of both oceanographers and meteorologists is to use weather data gathered by remote sensors and large-scale computers to increase our understanding of climate changes and improve climate forecasting.[33]

In May 1986, EOSAT (Landsat) and SPOT (System Probataire d'Observation de la Terre), by supplying pictures of the Soviet nuclear disaster at Chernobyl, made headlines around the world. SPOT, a combination of government and private interests in France, Belgium, and Sweden, was launched in February 1986, and proceeded to give the United States's EOSAT stiff competition in the business of providing high-quality photographs of Earth from space. SPOT can image objects on the ground as small as 33 feet (10 m), compared with EOSAT's resolution of 100 feet. Neither of these can compare with military spy satellites, which have resolutions in inches, but those images are not available to the public.

SPOT differs from EOSAT in that it uses charge-coupled device (CCD) technology and not scanners. As discussed on page 99, CCDs are an array of tiny sensors that measure the intensity of incoming light and convert it to electronic signals. Four of the CCD arrays used for high-resolution panchromatic images each have 6,000 sensors. SPOT can record up to 900,000 images a year that are sold at prices ranging from $155 to $2,550 per image, as compared with EOSAT prices of $50 to $3,300. SPOT is in 517-mile (832-km) high polar orbit. Because of

SPOT's battery limitations, it will have a life of around three years.

SPOT has caused some controversy, though. In the past, the primary buyers of commercial-space surveillance have been urban planners, scientists, farmers, and the like. SPOT has introduced a new user into the arena: the journalist. Sooner or later, a grouping of U.S. news organizations will try to launch their own satellite as a news-gathering eye in the sky. It could then be possible for the news media to reveal military buildups and if nations are lying about whether or not they are installing nuclear missiles. This will probably not occur soon, but the use of "space-cams" would pose a dilemma both to governments and news media alike.[34]

As powerful as these "space-cam" satellites are, their viewing power is nowhere as powerful as some countries' military surveillance satellites. As information about these satellites is classified, not much is known about them, and even some of the government agencies that direct and control these surveillance devices are cloaked in secrecy. The two major uses are to monitor arms-control agreements and guard against military buildups. We do know that there are two ways that images are acquired: (1) through the use of powerful conventional cameras and photographic film, and (2) by means of electro-optical scanning devices. In gathering information using film, the satellites take their pictures and then eject a container of exposed film toward Earth, to be picked up in midair by planes trailing wire rigging over the Pacific Ocean. This film is then brought to Washington, D.C., to be analyzed at the National Photographic Interpretation Center.

Newer surveillance satellites use electro-optical sensing devices to gather their images. Through the use of "folded optics," using mirrors to shorten the focal length, and CCDs, charge-coupled devices, a photo-conductive detector converts the image into digital data and transmits it back to Earth to be connected into an image. Additionally, the data transmitted are fed into a computer where they are enhanced or manipulated to bring out very faint images and then either viewed on a TV-like screen or transferred to photographic film.

Though the camera resolutions are highly classified, we do know that they are extremely powerful. It is said that they can read automobile license plates and distinguish between the clothing worn by soldiers and citizens. Their speed in transmission is awesome, too. Within an hour of imaging, let us say, troop movements in the Persian Gulf, that information can be at the White House.

Surveillance satellites have changed and will change how wars are fought. Today's military commander can direct troops in a real-time mode rather than relying on old information. The commander has the ability to maintain vital communication links and direct troop movement, monitor the troop movements of the opposition as they actually happen, and even, through the use of space lasers, bathe the battlefield at night with light visible to those equipped with special glasses. That satellites could be used as carriers of bombs is thought to be an ill-conceived notion by some, while some authorities believe that they could be used as destructive weapons of war, using laser systems that could destroy other satellites, missiles, and even Earth-based installations.[35]

The last of the eyes in the sky that have had scientific, military, and commercial applications is the navigation satellite. Although it was understood long before Sputnik that satellite-based navigation would be useful, Sputnik demonstrated the feasibility.

A problem of navigation for the U.S. Navy led to navigational satellites. The problem was that the inertial guidance system for the Polaris submarines exhibited unpredictable drift. Because these ships were on patrol for months at a time, a system was needed that would allow them to continue their patrol and not reveal their presence. The Applied Physics Laboratory at Johns Hopkins University set about to design a system of satellites to provide guidance for the submarine fleet, and the era of navigational satellites began. Today, navigational satellites are in orbit around the earth, servicing the military, mariners, and land surveyors. Fishing fleets, commercial-ship operators, and surveyors use their "Sat-Navs" to fix their positions and navigate. They pay a modest fee for the terminal and a monthly use fee. Even automakers are interested in applying these systems so that cars will have built-in navigators to tell you where you are and when to turn.[36]

THE FUTURE

Consider the fact that the technology that created the new eyes of the scientists is, for the most part, less than fifty years old. During the next fifty years, we will have a greater understanding of how our inner world works and of the physical laws that govern that inner world. We may be able to discover the systems that control our bodies and how to control those systems. With the new telescopes, we will be able to see some six billion light-years, to the very end of our universe. We may even drive cars that will never get lost or run into one another.

SOURCE NOTES

CHAPTER 1

1. Byron J. Ford, *The Revealing Lens* (London: George G. Harrop & Co., Ltd., 1973), pp. 11–67.
2. S. Bradbury, *The Evolution of the Microscope* (Oxford: Pergamon Press, 1963), pp. 305–314.
3. Saul Wischnitzer, *Introduction to Electron Microscopy*, Third Edition (New York: Pergamon Press, 1981), pp. 38–111.
4. Peter W. Hawkes, ed., *The Beginning of Electron Microscopy* (Orlando: Academic Press, 1985), pp. 3–6.
5. Theodore G. Rochow and Eugene G. Rochow, *An Introduction to Microscopy by Means of Light, Electrons, X-Rays, or Ultrasound* (New York: Plenum Press, 1978), pp. 3–8.

CHAPTER 2

6. Rochow, pp. 10–11.

7. John S. Hren and S. Ranganathan, eds., *Field-Ion Microscopy* (New York: Plenum Press, 1968), pp. 1–27.
8. Hawkes, pp. 53–54.
9. Rochow, pp. 319–332.
10. Julie Miller, "HVEM—The Big Picture of Small Structures." *Science News*, December 22, 1984, pp. 392–399.
11. Arthur L. Robinson, "Electron Microscope Inventors Share Nobel Physics Prize." *Science*, November 14, 1986, pp. 821–822.

CHAPTER 3

12. Euclid Seeram, *X-Ray Imaging Equipment* (Springfield, Ill.: Charles C. Thomas, 1985), pp. 7–27.
13. M. J. Brooker, *Computed Tomography for Radiographics* (Lancaster, England: MRP Press Limited, 1985), pp. 3–52.
14. Hans-Joachim Kretschmann and Wolfgang Weinrich, *Neuroanatomy and Cranial Computed Tomography* (Stuttgart: Georg Thieme Verlag, 1986), pp. 1–12.

CHAPTER 4

15. Sonny Kleinfield, *A Machine Called Indomitable* (New York: Times Books, 1985), pp. 119–242.
16. George K. Radda, "The Use of NMR Spectroscopy for the Understanding of Diseases." *Science*, August 8, 1985, pp. 640–645. Jean L. Marx, "Imaging Technique Passes Muster." *Science*, November 13, 1987, pp. 888–889.

CHAPTER 5

17. Howard Sochurek, "Medicine's New Vision." *National Geographic*, January 1987, pp. 2–41.
18. Isaac Asimov, *Eyes on the Universe* (Boston: Houghton Mifflin Company, 1975), pp. 1–262.
19. Stephen P. Maran, "A New Generation of Giant Eyes Gets to Probe the Universe." *Smithsonian* June 1987, pp. 40–53.
20. Edward Edelson, "Supernova." *Popular Science*, September 1987, pp. 60–64, 107.
21. John Holmes, "Surveying the Universe." *Insight*, June 22, 1987, pp. 8–17.
22. Leif Robinson, "Update: Telescopes of the Future." *Sky & Telescope*, July 1986, pp. 23–25.
23. Tim Beardsley, "Electric Eyes." *Scientific American*, September 1987, pp. 35–37.

CHAPTER 6

24. Mitchell M. Waldrop, "The New Art of Telescope Making." *Science*, December 1986, pp. 1495–1497.
25. Asimov, pp. 230–253.
26. Thomas Y. Canby, "Satellites That Serve Us." *National Geographic*, September 1983, pp. 280–335.
27. J. Kelly Beatty, "Voyager 2's Triumph." *Sky & Telescope*, October 1986, pp. 336–342.
28. George Abell, David Morrison and Sidney Wolff, *Exploration of the Universe* Fifth Edition (Philadelphia: Saunders College Publishings, 1987), pp. 180–212.
29. Abell, Morrison and Wolff, pp. 180–212.
30. J. Kelly Beatty, "Will Space Telescope Be Ready?" *Sky & Telescope*, February 1987, pp. 146–148.
31. John H. McElroy, ed., *Space Science and Applications* (New York: IEEE Press, 1986), pp. 3–5.
32. James P. Miller, "Satellites Are Growing Sharper at Spotting Mineral Deposits." *The Wall Street Journal*, April 3, 1987, p. 33.
33. McElroy, pp. 7–150.
34. Jim Schefter, "SPOT-ing Earth from Space." *Popular Science*, February 1987, pp. 78–81.
35. C. Kumar Patel and Nicolaas Blaembergen, "Strategic Defense and Directed-Energy Weapons." *Scientific American*, September 1987, pp. 39–45.
36. T. A. Heppenheimer, "Signaling Subs." *Popular Science*, April 1987, pp. 44–48.

INDEX

Abbe, Ernst, 16
Advanced X-Ray Astrophysics
  Facility
  see AXAF
Afterglow, 64
Alzheimer's disease, 67
Angel, Roger, 90
Angstrom, 18
Astronomy, 65, 90–91
Atoms, 11, 32, 37, 38, 49, 51, 66
AXAF, 122

Balloons, 107, 109, 120
Bias-resistor, 22
Binnig, Gerd, 50
Biostereomatics, 78–79
Birth defects, 76
Blood flow, 65–67, 78–79

Borra, Ermanno, 100
Brahe, Tycho, 83
Brain, 12, 55, 70

CAT, 55–56
Cathode-ray tube, 17, 29, 32, 67
  X-ray microscopy, 41
CCD, 93, 103, 105, 130–31
Charge-coupled device
  see CCD
Chromatic aberration, 84
Cloned antibodies, 81
Columbus Project, 105
Computed axial tomography
  see CAT
Computed transmission
  tomography
  see CTT

Computer tomography, 55–56, 58, 60–61
Computerized tomography
  see CT
Computer-aided tomagraphy
  see CAT
Coronary angioplasty, 66
Cosmic rays, 107, 122
Crookes tube, 53
CT, 55–56, 58, 59, 60–61, 63–65, 70–80
CTT, 55
Cyclotron, 66, 70

Daguerre, 125
Damadion, Raymond, 71
de Broglie, Louis, 17
Descartes, René, 15
Detectors, 63–64, 98, 117
Digital subtraction angiography
  see DSA
Doppler effect, 78
DSA, 65, 66
Dynamic spatial reconstructor, 61

Einstein Observatory, 108, 120
Electrical impedance, 79
Electron gun, 21, 22, 30
Electron microscope
  Development of, 16–18
  How they work, 21–24
  What can be seen, 24–25
Electron microscope microprobe analyzer
  see EMMA
Electron-field emission microscope, 33, 34
Electron-probe microanalyzer
  see EPMA
EM, 51
EMMA, 32
EPMA, 32, 40.
EOSAT, 126, 130

European Southern Observatory, 106
European Space Agency, 122
European Spacelab, 120

False images, 60
FEMs, 32, 33, 37
Fernandez-Moran, Humberto, 24
Fiber optics, 80–81
Field-emission microscopes
  see FEMs
Field-ion microscopes
  see FIMs
FIMs, 32, 36, 37, 38
Fluorescent imaging, 12

Galileo, 84, 117, 124
Gamma Ray Observatory, 122
Gamma rays, 67, 119, 122
Gantry, 55, 56, 58
Gas ionization, 63–64
Genes, 45, 52
Gerard P. Kuiper Airborne Observatory, 93, 118
Global Atmospheric Research Program, 130
Goddard, Robert, 109

Hale, George Ellery, 86–88
Halley's comet, 65
Hess, Victor, 107
High-voltage electron microscope
  see HVEMs
Hooke, Robert, 15
Hounsfield scale, 64
Hounsfield, Godfrey, 55
HST, 122–23
Hubble Space Telescope
  see HST
Hubble, Edwin, 122, 123
HVEMs, 45, 46, 47

IBM Research Laboratory, 49,
50
Imaging, 55, 60, 64, 66–67, 70,
76, 78–81
Infrared astronomy, 117–19
Infrared Astronomy Satellite
see IRAS
Interferometer, 105
Interferometry, 93
Intermediate-voltage electron
microscopes
see IVEMs
IRAS, 118, 119
Isotope americium, 55
IVEMs, 47

Jupiter, 84, 87, 112, 113, 114,
115, 116, 124

Keck Observatory, 102
Keck telescope, 100, 101, 103,
105
Kepler, Johannes, 15, 83, 90
Kitt Peak Observatory, 106
Kleinfield, Sonny, 66
Knoll, Max, 17
Kuiper Airborne Observatory,
93

Landsat, 126, 129, 130
Large Space Telescope
see LST
Las Campanas Observatory, 90,
105
Ley, Willie, 109
Lick Observatory, 84, 86
Limb darkening, 109
Lippershey, Hans, 83–84
LST, 122

Magellanic Cloud, 90, 105
Magnetic resonance, 71–76, 80
Magnetic resonance imaging
see MRI

Malpighi, Marcello, 15
Mariner, 111, 112, 113
Mars, 109, 111, 112, 117, 124
Mauna Kea, 100, 117–18
McMath Solar Telescope, 106
Medical imaging, 11, 12, 66, 71,
73, 75–76, 78
Metallurgy, 32, 37, 41, 51
Micrograph, 35, 37
Microscopes, 15, 16, 20, 22, 24–
25, 29, 36, 40, 42–44
Microscopy, 15, 16
Microsurgery, 81
Microwaves, 79
Milky Way, 84, 91
Mirror construction, 96–98
MMT, 103, 104
Mount Palomar, 88, 100
Mount Wilson, 87, 88
MRI, 71–76, 80
Müller, Erwin W., 32, 51
Multiple Mirror Telescope
see MMT

NASA, 65, 93, 118, 127–28
National Photographic Interpre-
tation Center, 131
Neurobiology, 47
Neutrinos, 95–96
New Technology Telescope
see NTT
Newton, Isaac, 84
NMR, 66, 71
NNTT, 103, 105
NTT, 106
Nuclear magnetic resonance
see NMR

Optical paths, 85
Optical telescope, 83–84, 96–
106
Orbiting Solar Observatory, 122

Palomar telescope, 123

PET, 66–67, 70, 80
Phasing, 97
Photodetectors, 43
Photographic plates, 98
Photomultiplier tube, 28, 63, 98
Photons, 28, 54, 98, 99, 122
Photo-conductive detector, 131
Picard, August, 107
Piezoelectric crystal, 76
Piezoelectric transducer, 42, 43
Pioneer, 112
Pixels, 65, 99
Pluto, 13
Polaroid, 28, 60
Positron emission tomography
  see PET
Protons, 39, 73
Proton-scattering microscope, 39
Pulsars, 93, 122

Quanta, 54
Quantum mechanics, 49–50
Quasars, 122

Radar, 80
Radiation, 39, 46
Radio pulse, 73
Radio telescopes, 97
Radio waves, 71, 73
Radioisotopes, 66
Radiology, 55
Reber, Grote, 91
Remote sensing, 125–26
Rockets, 109–10
Roentgen, William Konrad, 53, 54
Roentgenology, 54–55
Rohrer, Heinrich, 50
Royal Academy of Science, 50
Ruska, Ernst, 17, 18, 21, 23, 51
  Nobel Prize, 50

Sagittarius, 91
SAM, 42, 43, 44

Saturn, 11, 113, 115, 116, 124
Sat-Navs, 133
Scanners, 28, 61–62
Scanning acoustic microscope
  see SAM
Scanning electron microscope
  see SEM
Scanning laser acoustic
  microscope
  see SLAM
Scanning transmission electron
  microscope
  see STEM
Scanning tunneling microscope
  see STM
Sea ice, 128
Seasat, 128
Self-biased electron gun, 21
Self-biasing, 22
SEM, 28, 29, 30, 32
Shelton, Ian, 90–91, 95, 96
Single photon emission
  tomography
  see SPET
Single photon emission com-
  puter tomography
  see SPECT
SIRTF, 119
Skylab, 120
SLAM, 42
Slip bands, 37
Small Astronomy Satellite, 122
Solar Maximum Satellite, 120
Sonograms, 80
Sonography, 76
Space, 11, 107–24, 127–32
  Future, 133
  Neutrino astronomy, 95
  Remote sensing, 125–26
Space Infrared Telescope
  Facility
  see SIRTF
SPECT, 66, 67, 70
SPET, 67

SPOT, 130, 131
STEM, 30, 32
Stereoscopic images, 28
Stigmator lens, 18
STM, 49–52
Streaking, 60
Strong, John, 109
Superconducting electromagnets, 73
Superconductivity, 51
Superimposition, 97
Supernova, 90–91, 95, 96
Surveyor I, 111
Swammerdam, Jan, 15
System Probataire d'Observation de la Terre
    see SPOT

Telescopes, 11, 83–85, 87–89, 99, 108, 117, 121
    Radio, 91–96
    Venus, 109
TEMs, 19, 20, 21, 30, 41
    Limitations, 23, 27–28, 30
Thomson, Joseph J., 17
Tiros I, 129
Tomography, 56
Transducer, 76
Transmission electron microscope
    see TEMs
Tumors, 60, 81
Tungsten, 21, 30, 31
Tunneling, 49

Uhuru, 120
Ultrasound, 78
Ultraviolet, 119
Ulysses, 117, 123
Uranus, 11, 109, 115, 116

U.S. National New Technology Telescope
    see NNTT

Van Allen belts, 11
Van Allen, James, 110, 111
van Leeuwenhoek, Antoni, 16
Vega, 87, 118
Vela satellite system, 122
Venus, 84, 111, 125
Very Large Telescope
    see VLT
Very-long-baseline interferometry
    see VLBI
Video-scanning technique, 30
Viruses, 11, 41–42, 50, 52
VLBI, 93
VLT, 105
Voyagers, 114, 115–16, 124
von Braun, Wernher, 109–10

Wehnelt cylinder, 21
Wren, Christopher, 15

Xenon, 64
X-ray, 28, 32, 45, 53, 64, 65, 71, 76, 80
    Shortcomings, 55
    Types, 120
    Wavelengths, 39, 41, 54
X-ray microprobe analyzer, 41
X-ray microscopy, 39–42
X-ray telescope, 108
X-ray tube, 55, 63, 64

Yerkes Observatory, 84
Yerkes, Charles, 83

Zeiss, Carl, 16

Q
185.3
·M47
1988

#12.90